Journal
OF A DUTCH IMMIGRANT

FRANCIS RUITER

JOURNAL OF A DUTCH IMMIGRANT

Copyright © 2009 Francis Ruiter

ISBN-10: 1-926676-46-7
ISBN-13: 978-1-926676-46-3

Printed by Word Alive Press
131 Cordite Road, Winnipeg, MB R3W 1S1
www.wordalivepress.ca

I dedicate this book to
my wife Grace and three daughters,
LINDA, CAROLYN AND MARIANNE,
and my grandchildren.

TABLE OF CONTENTS

1

EARLIEST MEMORIES

April 13th, 1934, seven weeks before my fifth birthday, my cousin Peter Lieuwen and I were standing by Peter's parents' back door when Tante (aunt) Tryn came outside to tell us that Peter had a new brother. Tante Tryn was the 'Baker' in those days amongst our families, a formidable one at that, a no-nonsense type and a very hard worker skilled in her role. I asked our Tante if we would get a new brother in our family, too. "Yes, in a few weeks perhaps," she replied. At the age of five we were not conscious of our mothers' pregnancies. Babies came from heaven! Our youngest brother Gerrit, named after our father, was born on May 19, 1934.

My cousin Peter and I were best friends, spending a lot of time together in each other's homes. Our grandparents from my mother's side, the Lieuwens, lived across the street from Uncle Francis and Tante Lina Lieuwen, Peter's parents. This was about 100 meters from our home. Often we were invited by our aunties, Tante Tryn and Tante Ma, for a treat of milk and cookies or lemonade.

Their small home had two 'bed steden'. These were beds built along the wall of the living room, closed in with double doors giving the appearance of a clothes closet or cabinet when not in use. Sometimes we could sleep at our grandparents' house overnight. I don't know on what occasions, but I suspect the arrival of a new baby would have been one. I remember sleeping in the attic a few times, and more often after my Opa Lieuwen died.

My maternal grandfather, Jan Lieuwen (1854-1936), was born in Terschelling, an island just off the north coast of the province of Friesland. He had been a captain on sailing ships to such places as North America, England and Russia. However, in the early years of the 1900's, steamships were replacing sailing ships and he was laid off.

According to hearsay his last sailing ship he commanded came to an end on rocks along some coast. With the little savings he had, he started a small bakery on the island of Terschelling. My mother and her sisters needed to sell bread and buns in the village to help stay in business.

My mother met my father when she left the island for Andyk (my birthplace) to work as domestic help. Her brother Frans followed, then the two sisters and, finally, our grandparents, the Lieuwens.

Opa Lieuwen, then in his mid-seventies, would sometimes do work for his son, Francis, my uncle. Opa Lieuwen was a bit temperamental at times and did not relate very well to his grandchildren. One time cousin Peter and I, knowing his temper, decided to tease him a little. He was cleaning some wooden potato flats, scraping mud off them with a jack-knife. I don't remember how we went about getting him upset, but he threw his jack-knife at us. What rascals we were! We were seven years old at the time.

Opa died that same year, at the age of 82. One morning at breakfast my father told me that Opa Lieuwen had gone to heaven. I said, "No! He can't be gone like that!" I had seen him just a few days before. My father said, "Come along with me and I will show you". There in his home he lay, all dressed up and stretched out on his bed, ready for burial. He looked peaceful. Then I realized he did not leave this earth physically but spiritually.

Grandmother Lieuwen lived a number of years yet. As she was becoming very deaf, we needed to shout for her to understand us.

Our aunts were the most humble and thankful people I encountered in my life. They would sometimes invite us for lunch, especially if we did some work around the yard, cutting the grass or shearing the hedge. They would treat us with cookies and lemonade or 'prakkie', fried potatoes with a lightly browned crust. We loved it. There was always a simple prayer for any food eaten, even for a piece of cake at tea: "Thank you, Lord, for the food we will consume". I was never eager to do these little chores for my aunts, but my father would point out that they did so much for others and that they would be so thankful. We liked the way they expressed their thanks.

Pete Lieuwen and I were staunch friends. We always walked to school together, a distance of about one kilometre. One day in grade three, on the way to school, we noticed an attractive garden along the side of the road. There were some young carrots the size of our finger, and we decided to pick a few for a taste test. Since some mud clung to them we brought them to school intending to clean them in the washroom. Upon arriving at the main entrance, the principal saw us carrying those carrots and asked us where we got them. We simply told him that we picked them from a garden along the road to school. Well now! He called it stealing and we were told to return them to the owner and apologize, which we did. The woman that answered the doorbell chuckled and said, "That is okay boys, don't worry about it". In our childish minds, we, who were brought up with gardens and fields of produce, found it ridiculous to be accused of stealing. After all, carrots from amongst plenty were as normal as rain from heaven.

I was eleven when the Second World War broke out in our country of Holland. It was the 10th of May, and my father took me along to plant beans in a small field behind the 'boerderij (farmstead). We saw a few airplanes streaking through the sky and it was explained to me that the German Nazi regime had invaded Holland. Furthermore, it would not be many days before our country was over-run. The German army would bring us into subjection, and we would lose our rights. In my mind, it was useless to plant beans when the occupying forces might take them away. Of course, I was thinking of an excuse to avoid the task of crawling on my knees in the dirt and planting. My father answered that we should not stop working nor give up hope for the future. We would all have to eat!

A few years into the war, shortages became apparent. Young people would crave sweets and goodies. Many articles became very scarce or not available, such as oranges, bananas and lemons.

One time the milk delivery truck passed by as we walked home from school. I noticed a container of 'karnamelkse pap' (barley cooked in buttermilk) on the truck and the tap was protruding over the edge. I thought I would like to taste it. When the milkman stopped for a delivery, I quickly opened the tap and let some of the stuff pour into my hand slurping it in. My school friends thought it funny but did not try it themselves.

By 1944, supplies really got scarce; everything was rationed. My cousin Pete and I knew every nook and cranny of our parents' warehouses. We knew that the underground resistance movement was storing certain food items to supply families harbouring refugees. We discovered cheeses among potato flats, and flour. We found butter under the floorboards. There was a crockpot I had passed several times, which I thought contained salt. I discovered one day, by sticking a wet finger into it, that it was sugar. What a discovery! I couldn't believe it. Sometimes we would take a slice of cheese, other times we mixed butter with flour and sugar. Oh, how delicious that tasted! We were skinny teen-agers by that time of the war.

One time, in the attic of Uncle Francis's warehouse, we discovered a section, blocked off with tulip crates, which seemed strange to us. We went down one floor where there was a trap door in the ceiling. We piled up some empty crates in order to reach the ceiling, opened that trapdoor and were utterly amazed to see hundreds of sausages hanging on racks to dry and mature. The underground had raided a sausage factory and had stored them there. We sliced the sausage into bite size pieces but it was raw, uncured. We never talked about our discoveries to our siblings or friends. We knew this was contraband stuff, not to be talked about with anyone.

At age 14, we attended junior high school in Enkhuizen about 10 km from our homes. We biked there everyday, come wind, rain or shine. When there was a strong headwind, we would sometimes bike in an angle formation. The person in front broke the wind; the next person would put his right hand on the shoulder of the person in front and so on, giving each other support. Another way to beat the wind was to hitch a ride from a delivery truck, which I did on one occasion when the driver stopped to make a delivery on the edge of town. When he started to move, I grabbed a loose rope on the left side at the rear of the truck. The trucks in 1943 (war time) could not go very fast; with no gasoline they ran on butane, a gas derived from burning coal briquettes. Maximum speed was about 50-60 km per hour. When the driver took off along the dyke road to Andyk and noticed me in his rearview mirror, he tried to lose me by driving on the left side of the road close to the soft grassy shoulder. There were some large milk cans standing on the edge of the road that dairy farmers put there for pickup. The truck driver thought he would get rid of me by driving close to those milk cans. I managed to get around them quick enough to grab the rope again, but after doing this twice I realized the danger and gave up.

Another time I was smarter. When the driver made a delivery, I quickly put my bike and myself in the back of the truck behind the canvas cover and rode along until his first stop in our village. When the driver saw me coming out from behind the canvas he was nonplussed and muttered something about the law, but let me go.

I left junior high at age 15 and started to work for my father's seed business and in horticulture.

The last year of the war affected me in various ways. At the age of 15-16 I was very impressionable. We often heard and saw large formations of bomber planes overhead. Sometimes dogfights between German and Allied planes took place, often during the night. I was a sound sleeper, but I wanted to see these aerial fights and asked my dad to wake me up when the next fight was on. The next night he woke me up and I heard the guns blazing and airplanes screaming in the air. I listened a while and it scared me very much. I told my dad never to wake me again; it was too frightening.

During our summer vacation of 1944, some friends and I were camping in the bush next to a farmyard. We helped the farmer with the threshing and baling of straw. One afternoon, we looked up to see a formation of bomber planes heading to Germany. All of a sudden we saw one fighter plane leave the formation and come down, seemingly straight at us. We dove under the straw bales, terrified. We heard shooting, and when we came from under the bales we saw smoke about 400 meters away where an automobile was ripped through with bullets.

One of the strongest memories I have of the war is of Amsterdam, near the end, when I was sent by bike to bring food to our relatives. The once lively Amsterdam looked so forlorn with hungry people eating whatever was available. My cousin, Peter Kapteyn, took me to a soup kitchen for a meal of sugar beet pulp, but we were interrupted by air attack sirens. We hid in a bomb shelter until the all clear was given.

I had loved going to Amsterdam by bicycle to visit my cousin Peter there. We would explore side streets amid the hustle and bustle of the market. He liked to take us to a cinema to see a newsreel and a cartoon, which cost a dime. Sometimes we managed a movie by bribing the porter with a nickel to get into the theatre where the minimum age was sixteen. Movie houses were forbidden territory, not only because of the age factor, but also because we were Christian children.

This time, in the spring of 1945 just before the war was over, I was glad to return home from Amsterdam. I felt depressed by the sights along the road. I saw many people looking for, if not begging or trading personal belongings for, food. They walked or rode bicycles on solid rubber tires made out of discarded auto tires. Their clothing was bedraggled, and their facial expressions showed devastation.

These experiences and images have stayed with me until now. I often dreamed to be free, and able to fly high above, the earth—to distance myself from possible bombing attacks, or just to escape earthly problems that seemed impossible to solve. For many years, sirens from fire trucks, police cars or ambulances would send a chill down my spine.

A few years after the war, I moved out of adolescence. I consciously decided I would do my share in the work that had to be done around the seed business or in the field. I liked to work with horses in the field: ploughing, harrowing, seeding or harvesting. I had grown up and I took responsibility for the tasks at hand. Two years later, in the spring of 1948, I emigrated, with two other cousins, to Canada.

2

LOEVESTEIN

Loevestein: the home where I was born in 1929, as a scrawny little runt, in a small village called Andijk, situated along the Zuider Zee about 50 km north of Amsterdam.

The name Loevestein was painted above the entrance of our home, in white letters on a green background, just below the eaves troughs. It was a reference to a Castle in the south of Holland.

Andijk was divided by two main roads going east and west, one km apart, for a distance of about 5 km. In between were parcels of land separated by canals. These parcels of land were further subdivided, and individual farmers had their own plots where they grew flowers, such as tulips and gladiolas, and other horticultural crops.

Our home was located on the south road. Built around 1918, it was not as ostentatious as a real castle; nevertheless, it housed as many as fourteen persons. There was a spacious bathroom on the second floor, in which we had a claw foot bathtub, two washbasins and a toilet. There was hot and cold running water throughout the house.

In front of our home were some low shrubbery and perennial flowers, and our home was separated from the street by a Cole aster hedge.

On the east side of our home was a lawn where lines held the weekly wash. I remember, too, that in the middle of the lawn, we had an old Model T Ford in which I could play, pretending to drive a car. The rear of our house was separated from the warehouse, where my father had his office, by a gravel courtyard about twenty feet wide. In the middle of this courtyard was a swing set, on which I managed to bloody my knees on several occasions.

Our home was separated from the neighbours' by a wooden wall and a lean-to roof spanning our home and the warehouse. A sturdy tin roof covered the buildings. This was where we stored our bicycles and the wooden shoes we used in the fields when planting or weeding. Alongside that roof was a water pipe that I could reach by jumping up. I would get a hold of the pipe and then swing myself onto the tin roof. When I was sixteen to seventeen years old, this was how I snuck into my bedroom upstairs, after 10 p.m. when the back door was locked for the night. I used to make sure my bedroom window was not locked in case I was late coming home, as I did not want to meet my dad in his long johns at the back door. Coming home late was not a way to improve his mood. He did not like his sleep interrupted after rising early and working hard all day.

At the back entrance of the house, there was a toilet and a short hallway where we hung our outer clothes. Behind a partition, there was a storage area for winter supplies of canned goods, as well as a washing machine, and a pump to draw rainwater from an underground storage tank.

From the back hall we entered a large kitchen and eating area. The table in the middle of the room could seat twelve persons. The kitchen had a large woodstove, but we usually used briquettes. Beside the stove was a cellar door where, besides perishable items, some berry wine was kept. Of course, I needed to taste it when my mother was out of sight.

When my mother was cooking, the aromas wafted through the room, making my mouth drool. My father would sit at the end of the table, with me and two older, muscular brothers next to him. Jan was on his right, I was on his left, and Herman was next to me.

My Dad humoured me to keep me quiet and to prevent me from trying to get away from my chair. He and my two older brothers did not appreciate interference when they were discussing business. If I misbehaved too much I was asked to sit for a while in the closet just behind the table. No one was allowed to leave the table until my father read a Bible verse and said a short prayer.

I was number ten in the line up of twelve siblings, seven of them girls. During my teen years, three of these girls were employed away from home. If conversation between my other sisters, who were sitting on my mother's side of the table, became a bit boisterous—my sister, Joke, with her musical voice reached particularly high notes—my Dad would ask them to pipe down. If they paid no attention, he would throw his damp finger cloth in their face. It worked, for we had great respect for our Dad.

To enter the living room you had to cross the front porch. This porch was scrubbed every week together with all the windows. The porch had one step and was accessible by a stone walk from the road. This same roadway was where my older sister, Tine, pushed me--a thin one year old--in a stroller to get some needed vitamin "D".

The living room was quite spacious, large enough to hold a table for fifteen. It was kept warm throughout the winter by a hearth and a coal stove. We needed that living room space during the war when we kept refugees, or out-of-town family members, in our home. In one corner we had an organ that my older brother and sister could play.

On Sundays my sisters occasionally brought a few girl friends home from church. After dinner they often would sing popular songs accompanied by the organ. I enjoyed the singing, too, and would frequently join them.

On the other side of the room were two clothes closets, one in each corner, separated by a window. In one closet my dad kept his dress suit. This included a vest in which he kept some small change. I found this interesting and, at times, when I felt a need for sweets or gum, I stole a few nickels or dimes from my dad's vest pocket. (This was in the mid thirties when there was little money for treats and there were so many of us who had to share whatever food and goodies were available). Of course I got caught and was given a talking to about stealing. I remember the tears in my dad's eyes.

Adjacent to the living room was our parents' bedroom, which included an extra hideaway bed for one person. There were times when we were overrun by so many guests that my younger brother, Gerrit, and I had to share this small bed. Near the hearth my Mother had her favourite chair. When I was young and felt sick or lonely I would seek her lap to cuddle up in and be consoled.

To reach the second floor you climbed a steep and narrow set of stairs from the kitchen. One time, in a hurry, I took a run at the stairs and hit my head on the entrance ceiling. Ouch! I got a big bump on my head.

There were four bedrooms on the second floor. One was a large room with two double beds and a sofa, which could accommodate five persons if needed. It was called "the girls' room" as it was for the women in our family. The next one, painted green and therefore called "the green room", had one double bed. My brother Herman slept there. I and my brother Gerrit usually slept in a double bed in what was called the "blue room". (Yes, the walls were blue.) It was not very private, because the way to the main bathroom led right through it. Behind the bathroom was brother Jan's single bedroom called the "pink room". We always referred to the rooms by their respective names.

During the war years an extra bed was put in place in the attic, for use when we were overloaded with guests or refugees. This happened frequently, although an older brother, together with a few refugees, often slept in a hideaway place in the warehouse.

(Towards the end of the war and later, there were times I had nightmares about being picked up by soldiers who, now and then, tried to recruit men, by force, to work in German war factories.)

Throughout it all, I would say we had a warm and cohesive family. We shared our home with many a visitor who enriched our lives during these often difficult times.

3

ELEMENTARY SCHOOL YEARS

I was born in Holland in 1929 into a family of 12 children, 7 girls and 5 boys. I was number 10.

Our town was a small village of about 1500 inhabitants near the Zuider Zee. The Zuider Zee is really a lake now, since 1932 when the large dyke was built to close off this large inlet from the North Sea. The dyke holds the water from flooding the lowlands. It is about 5 km long with crossroads spaced about every half kilometre.

Our village was called Andijk. It got its name from the way the town was built adjacent to the dyke. We lived about one kilometre south of the Zee, which runs parallel to the dyke. Our Christian school was built along the dyke as well, about one km from our home.

As youngsters we always walked to school. My cousin Peter, who lived kitty corner from our place, would join me each morning. We carried a cotton pouch to hold our lunch, which we ate under the supervision of our teachers. We wore short pants, knee-high stockings and thin leather slippers that fit into our shoes. Most times we wore wooden shoes. They were comfortable and warm in winter. During the winter we wore tall knitted stockings, held up with garter belts. I hated those stockings. They were itchy and forever got holes in them from falls.

On our way home from school there was more time to linger or to explore things. If you had a penny, which was significant during the depression years, you might stop at the corner store for some liquorice. Of course, there so many different candies and chocolates displayed that a young boy would look at all of it with desiring eyes. One time it so happened that I had a penny to spend. I recalled someone suggesting that, when the store clerk turns around, you should snatch an extra treat from the counter. I fell for the idea, but got caught red-handed. I was deeply ashamed, and it cured me from trying that again.

Another incident happened in grade four. I was chewing gum in class. It was rather a big clod of gum from too many Chiclets in my mouth and I did not know how to get rid of that sticky stuff. (Nowadays children would stick it under their seats.) When my teacher saw me with a mouth full of something, he asked me to take it out, and out came a wad of gum. He told me to wrap it up in some paper and deposit it in the waste basket. The teacher then asked me to stay after school. He questioned me as to how I got the gum, since this was during the depression (1938) and no one had money to buy gum. I would have liked to lie. However, I was just not good at it. If I tired to fabricate a story it never worked. Having no way out, I meekly told my teacher that I had snatched a nickel from my Dad's vest pocket, which was stored in his clothes closet. The teacher, who later became my brother-in-law, told me he would not speak of it to my parents, but I had to promise not to do it again. In hindsight, it was a good learning experience; it helped me to stay honest in future years.

In grade five things got tougher for me. At the Christian school I attended, we were expected to learn many verses from the Psalms by heart. Memorizing Psalm verses was not my strong point.

If you could not recite the assigned verse for the day, you would be penalized by having to stay after school and work at it. Of course I was one of the culprits and had to find a way around this problem.

I solved it in a daring way. My school bench was in the front row up against the teacher's desk. His desk was about 6 inches higher than my bench. For some reason—maybe to keep a close watch on me—he would seat himself beside me. However, he sat on top of the desk with his feet on the seat, facing the facing the other students and not me. Since his eyes were on my classmates, and he was looking away from me, I put my Psalm book against his teacher's desk and beside his rump, so I could read the verse that I was to recite. My classmate behind me saw it and snickered.

In grade six, things got really hot. My teacher was an ex-army sergeant, a strict disciplinarian. I had a difficult time with him and lost self-esteem, due to the degrading manner in which he treated me for no good reason. I admit I was a playful person. I could take punishment when warranted, but, when accused of something that was not my doing, I felt terribly hurt.

One day in class, when our teacher was haranguing us about studying and having our homework completed in time, I felt a pang of guilt. I voluntarily admitted guilt in that regard and was about to explain that I had remedied the situation, but oh, no. Before I could explain my amendment, he went into a tirade and humiliated me in front of my class. Then he made me stay after class, took me to the attic woodworking shop and browbeat me some more. It was so bad; I was ready to kick him from the top of the stairs from where we were standing.

When I came home that day, I told my dad in no uncertain terms that I was finished with school. I explained what had taken place. He listened to me and when I was finished my story he calmly said, "OK, tomorrow you work with me."

For the next three days he worked me hard. I almost had second thoughts about quitting school. However, I knew he was testing me and did not complain.

After three days, the teacher came to our home and asked my father, in my presence, why I was not attending school. My father turned the question around and asked the teacher, "Why is it that he is very unhappy with you and refuses to go to school?" After some babble, he let out that I was lazy. At that, my father interjected and said, "That cannot be true, because he worked with me for three days and is certainly not lazy." I knew then that I had won my argument about the teacher's teaching methods. I had gained new respect for my father who did not accept someone else's word out of hand. I went back to school and kept my guard up around that teacher until the end of the term.

4

MY PARENTS

Gerrit Ruiter (1888—1982) Born in Opperdoes, Holland
Alida Lieuwen (1890—1977) Born in Terschelling, Holland

Our parents loved us, their twelve children, and we loved them in return. (I was number ten in the line-up.) They were good to us, despite their busy lives. Our father was an early riser, often doing some fieldwork before breakfast. The rest of us came down later, ready for school, and joined him for breakfast.

Father was a very busy man, managing a seed company as well as farming quite a bit of land. We grew vegetables for seed, plus potatoes and tulip bulbs. (My two older brothers became active in the business later. My oldest brother was in charge of the agricultural side; the other was in the warehouse where the vegetable seeds were processed by cleaning, and grading prior to packaging and shipment to retailers.) He was very organized. Besides looking after his business and his family, he worked actively in the community. As a church elder he attended many meetings. All this activity left him little time to play with his children. Later, after he retired, he confessed to me that he regretted this.

Even though my dad did not spend a lot of time with us, I felt he showed a lot of patience with me. If there was a misdemeanour on my part he would always hear me out before passing judgment. It happened a couple of times that I took some coins from his Sunday suit pockets to buy gum or sweets. When I was found out the first time, he explained to me that stealing was wrong and admonished me with some stern talk.

Some time later I did it again. My father was grieved by my repeat offence and at a loss for how to handle his boy. He was so disappointed by my action that he got tears in his eyes trying to convince me of the seriousness of stealing. He talked about what it will do to a person and the eventual consequences of that. I did not think that the few coins I had taken required my father's tears. I loved my father and did not want to see him sad.

Despite his busy schedule, Father did occasionally manage to take his younger children to the beach of a summer day. Mother wore a short-sleeved bathing suit, but stayed on the beach. For treats, we had oranges and peanuts, a real feast in those days!

My parents loved each other dearly. They were different in nature but there was a mutual respect for each other's role in life

I know I was difficult to handle and easily bored. He would take me along sometimes on short business trips, so my mother could pay more attention to my two younger siblings. Father would take me along when he went to see farmers to discuss contracts for growing vegetable seeds or to inspect those fields for yields and purity. I liked those outings during summer vacation. I was bored when his dealings with farmers took too long, but. I enjoyed the rides through the countryside. We drove a Plymouth in the early thirties and, in the late thirties; he traded it for a German car, an Opel. My father was mostly in the foreground in life, through business and community. My mother was very supportive by managing the household and fulfilling her role as 'mother hen'. She was not interested in the limelight.

Mother made the meals, repaired our clothes, and saw us to bed. She had a full-time helper for some years. Later my eldest sister, Nelly, took over. Nelly was a conscientious and efficient worker, almost like a second mother. She sacrificed her young life to assist mother, so that her younger sisters, six of them, could stay in school longer and have careers. Nelly finally got engaged at age 33 and we were very happy for her. Anyway, even though I had two younger siblings, Carolina and Gerrit, I did not lack my mother's attention and affection. Whenever I had a problem—whether I was unhappy or not feeling well—I could crawl into her lap for comfort. She understood my temperament and would handle me with compassion. Sometimes she had to be stern, other times just a few words of advice. Once, I remember, she could not help but smile through her look of rebuke when I sneaked into the kelder, the cold cellar, and tasted some homemade berry wine. If things really got out of hand I was referred to my father's office for a stronger reprimand or punishment. Sometimes I would have to make restitution when something got broken.

Mother also gave words of encouragement when my older siblings put me down. I matured slowly, being too playful. My older brothers, in particular, would complain about me not sharing the workload to their expectation. Mother once made the remark, "Give him time. Hij word nog weleens wat." (He will become someone in his own right someday.) I kept this in mind in the future, at times when I felt some doubt.

Sex was not discussed in our home, but, when I got older and started dating, father gave advice on kuisheid (purity). Essentially this meant keeping your pants on and not groping. My father and mother showed affection for each other, not in a demonstrative way, but in subtle or spontaneous ways. For example, I saw my mother helping Dad with his shirt tie and saw them smiling after a comment about vanity. Father always gave her a hug and a kiss on the cheek when leaving on a business trip and when returning home. He would do the same with relatives he went to visit or who came to visit us; he would show affection with a hug and/or kiss. Most relatives were endeared to my father by receiving advice from him or perhaps a loan.

Father was also a good public speaker. He was often asked to read sermons in church because of his clear voice and good diction. He gave several speeches, the most memorable of which were just after the war: He greeted the Canadian liberators with a short speech when they arrived in our town. Later, he delivered a well-received speech at the unveiling of a statue to remember the dead and to honour workers in the underground. He also gave a most astounding speech on May 5, 1977, at the age of 89, when he was nearly blind. This last public speech was about 1600 words spoken from memory while my brother John stood behind him with a written copy. It was at the unveiling of a replacement statue, a very emotional speech, which left some people in tears. When I reread the review of this occasion I still get tears in my eyes. The theme of his speech was written on the stone, "Verberg de verdrevene en vermeld de omzervende niet." (Conceal the refugees and do not expose the wandering.)

My father was 86 years old in 1974 when I made one of my periodic visits to Holland from Canada (where I have lived since my immigration in1948). Father invited me to drive him to Den Helder, a strategic port city some 50 km north of my parent's home. It had a naval base protecting the inlet between the North Sea and the inland Zuider Zee with its 16th &17th century ports. During the First World War he was stationed there in a stone bastion at the seaside. The fort was adjacent to the large town square on which were a number of cafes and restaurants.

I knew my father as a sober person who did not drink hard liquor, did not swear and did not seem to have had the faults some of us experienced in our younger lives. Standing in the square, looking towards the cafes, I asked him if he ever imbibed at those watering holes with his army buddies in those days. I thought surely he must have had some weaknesses in his younger years. He answered, no, he hadn't; they used to have Bible studies in the evenings. I was amazed and felt some remorse about my own past delinquencies. He was a man of courage, dignity and piety.

My father was also a man of peace and one who gave credit where credit was due. We often entertained guests and it was our custom to sing a Psalm after dinner. One time a guest had a very scratchy voice but sang with gusto. We young people later made some unflattering comment about this guest's singing. My father responded, "Remember, he loves to sing God's praises, too!" That made us shut up! He always tried to see the best in other people. I was never able to emulate him in this regard.

I still give thanks to God for both of my parents who showed what it is like to have strong ethics and faith in God.

5

GOING TO CHURCH (1935)

Our church in Holland was about one kilometre walk from where we lived and—sun, rain or frost—we never missed a Sunday service. Our large family would take up most of a bench on the balcony. When we became adolescents we occasionally sat with friends. Until then, we all sat together.

Our parents, in their fifties, would go by car and give a ride to our elderly grandparents. The rest of us would walk. The churchgoers would come from two directions, from the south and the north, like a long parade, two or three abreast. Those living farther away often used their bicycles.

Our church in Andijk was built in 1929/1930, an architectural beauty with stained glass windows depicting Biblical scenes. It had central heating and a seating capacity of 1100 persons. The lectern was set on a spacious elevated platform, which could be reached by a set of stairs on either side. Overhanging the platform was a large pipe organ, very picturesque with all the shining pipes facing the congregation. The lighting consisted of a well-placed chandelier, about five meters long, hanging from the ceiling. I tried counting the individual lights many times but never got the same number.

On either side of the podium was a row of benches, one side reserved for elders and the other side for deacons. When the deacons and elders

The church in Andijk, North Holland.

were seated, dressed up in their dark blue suits, they looked very official. At strategic places on the balcony, two benches were reserved for the deacons who handled the collections.

Most seats in the church were reserved for families. Five minutes before the church service started the church council entered from a side door. Then a red light would go on to signal that any reserved seats not yet occupied were now available for general seating.

After the opening liturgy and a few songs, it was customary to have an elder read the Ten Commandments from a smaller lectern in front of the platform. One elderly elder, in his turn, spoke in the local dialect, which amused many.

When the pastor started the sermon, my mother opened her purse and handed out peppermints to us youngsters to keep us quiet. The first part of the sermon would last about 20 minutes. Then a song was introduced and everyone was asked to rise, presumably to keep the sleepy people awake. After that, the sermon continued for another 10 minutes. It was rough going for young people who were not interested what the pastor had to say. However, we were well trained. Sometimes, when a sermon

19

lasted longer, my mother handed out an extra peppermint to keep us happy a little longer.

If a youngster got out of line and became a bit boisterous, an elder would quickly dispatch himself and let the child know that, if he did not behave himself, he would be sent packing. If the misbehaving young-ster's parents were also in attendance you could be sure he or she would be dealt with sternly at home.

As I mentioned, everyone walked to church except those that lived too far away and elderly people who could get a ride from someone with an automobile.

I, too, wanted a ride in my father's car, but he would not let me. When I was about 9 years old my dad bought a new car made in Ger-many called an Opel. It had a good-sized trunk in the back. I wondered if I could fit in that trunk and get a ride home. While Dad was having a dis-cussion with somebody, I quickly climbed in the trunk, keeping the lid open just a slit to see what was going on. When my Father started the car and drove away with my mother and aunts, I opened the lid a bit more and waved to my friends. Other folks saw me too, of course, and got a great kick out of it. I don't think I got punished for it, maybe just a rep-rimand. Some people might have considered it bad behaviour; you could have fun during the weekdays but not on Sundays.

My dad was not an authoritarian type of person; he could be patient and consider the circumstances. One winter Sunday morning the road was icy and the canals were frozen solid. I challenged my father, sug-gesting that I go to church on skates. In those days most parishioners would have frowned upon such a worldly act. He did not bat an eye and said, "Why, sure, go ahead." I think he reasoned to himself, Francis wants to use the icy roads as an excuse to stay home. Let him go. My siblings were astonished and envious to see me putting on skates while they had to walk. In reflecting on churchgoing in my youth, I realize that my Father was a wise man. He could be stern, but he was compassionate, and in this way he taught me discipline and sound judgment.

6

ANGST

It was the fall of 1944, the final year of the Second World War. The days were becoming shorter and darker. The Canadian Army, in their push northward, was stopped at the Rhine River in the Netherlands. Despite the efforts of the British crack paratroops, their glider planes loaded with soldiers and ammunition, they were not able to secure the bridge across the Rhine. The drop zone was too far from its objective; a German panzer division lay between the Allied forces and the bridge.

This made the days grimmer in the northern part of Holland. Cut off from adequate food supplies, especially in the larger cities such as Amsterdam, people suffered from starvation and malnutrition.

I was fifteen years old at the time. Where we lived, in a farming area 50 km north of Amsterdam, we had enough to eat. Although there was little or no meat, our bellies were being filled with potatoes, cabbage, turnips and carrots. Still, by the following spring I was skinny as a runt, the outline of my rib cage clearly visible beneath my skin. Still, we had enough food and were happy to share it with relatives in the city. Several times I was sent by my father as a courier on bicycle to bring them some supplies.

While we were free of hunger, we were not secure from the secret service of the German occupation forces. In our village, we were harbouring several hundred refugees. Some were former Dutch soldiers and others refugees who would have been recruited for the German war machine as labourers.

My father, who operated a wholesale seed business with a number of employees, headed an organization to place these refugees with different families in our village of about 5000 inhabitants. In our home, we had one to three refugees staying with us at any given time.

Our dinner table held as many as 14 persons, including the guests. It was extended with a sheet of plywood, one end resting on the main table, the other end on a smaller table.

My mother and oldest sister were the main "worker bees" in our home. We also had two spinster aunts living next door who would peel a bucketful of potatoes for lunch and another for supper. There was not enough grain to make all the bread we needed, only enough for breakfast and a lunch for the field workers. Fortunately, we had enough winter vegetables, besides potatoes.

We also had a lot of dried beans and peas from our gardens. Saturdays we usually ate peas—large wrinkled ones (a kind not grown in Canada)—with some cubes of fried suet; other days maybe some navy beans with a sliver of ham, and a potato.

Shortly after the German army had overrun Holland, Hitler had allowed the prisoners of war to return home. (This included my oldest brother.) Hitler reasoned that by this gesture he would gain the trust of the Dutch population and they would accept his ideals. It did not work; the people did not cooperate. When the ex-prisoner soldiers were called to return to their former barracks, some men did return, and a few even joined the German army, but most went into hiding.

One of our earliest guests during the war had been an officer in the Dutch army. We called him Johnny. He had false identity papers, as did every other underground person we had in our village. Our Johnny stayed with us for a couple of years until it got too dangerous for him to stay. Someone had reported Johnny to the secret police. By the time they came to our home to arrest him, he had already flown the coop. Searching for him in vain, they did find a smoked ham in the attic, which they considered contraband (probably true) and confiscated. We had two other underground guests with us and we were afraid the soldiers would check their identity and take them away. My father was not home at the time, and our family, frightened, huddled up in the living room waiting to see what would happen. Fortunately, the soldiers seemed content with finding the ham; no doubt their own diet did not include such a delicacy.

A few days later, however, my father was ordered to appear before the German police, charged with harbouring an ex-soldier. He pleaded not guilty, informing them that he had simply hired this man for his expertise in bookkeeping. Father told them that Johnny had left some time ago and he did not know his whereabouts. After some grilling they let father go, but a few days later he was ordered to report back and was immediately incarcerated. He was told that they would keep him until the ex-officer reported to them. We were very worried about his safety and prayed for his release.

Through the underground organization, which helped men seeking refuge in our village, word got out to our Johnny. Johnny respected my father very much because of his heavy involvement in the underground. He realized the importance of my father's freedom to the overall cause of the resistance movement. He reported to the German police and my father was released. Johnny became a prisoner of war for some months, but was released when a doctor in our village administered some medication which gave him the appearance of having pleurisy.

The secret police were not finished with my Dad, however. They became aware of the underground organization he was involved in. It harboured ex-army men and other young men who did not report for duty for the war machine. One day, just when it was getting dark, they came for my father again with an army paddy wagon.

We were all sitting around the dinner table waiting for my dad to join us. Suddenly, a loud knock shook the door and soldiers rushed in, carbine rifles in hand, their heavy boots pounding in the hall. It scared us near to death. The house was surrounded, and no one could leave to sound the alarm. The officer in charge asked my mother where my father was. Somewhat flustered, my mother, "I don't know."

"Does your husband not tell you where he goes?" he demanded.

"Why yes, he just has not shown up," she replied.

They searched our home and the warehouse behind. We were worried that he would come home and fall into the trap. While checking the house, one of the soldiers had left his rifle leaning in the corner of the room right behind my chair. I sat there, sweating, on my chair. Everyone was quiet, waiting to see what would transpire. My thoughts were still on the gun: Was it loaded? Would I dare pick it up? I realized, Then do what? Probably not even loaded. We had underground refugee guests around the table, but no one was asked for their identity. We had left our food untouched; no appetite for the moment.

After a fruitless search the soldiers left. With a sigh of relief, we wondered what happened to our dad. It so happened that my father had been visiting a neighbour a little way down the road. Returning home in the falling darkness, he saw movement in the front of our home. Realizing something was amiss, he turned around, walked away and stayed hidden with an other neighbour.

From there on we did not see Father for about three months. He roamed around the province, staying with friends and an old aunt of his. Now and then a message was sent to my mother that all was well with him. My mother always appeared calm and trusted God to protect her husband. My two older brothers carried on with the business at hand. About a month before the war ended, my father returned home. By then the local German detachments were more worried about their own safety and did not bother us any more.

On the last day of the war, my Dad put me to work in the garden across the road from our home. He was concerned about me joining a group of rowdy young men who anticipated there would be an announcement that the war was over, and might take part in revelry and vandalism.

And so the war came to an end. My last memory was of a lone soldier walking past our home carrying his carbine. I heard him mumble again and again "My kameraad, my kameraad." I guess he lost his best friend. He looked sorrowful and defeated. I thought he was searching for his army unit, which was about 6 miles away. I realized then that he was probably a soldier conscripted against his will. I felt sorry for him.

7

JOY RIDES

I was sixteen years old after World War II ended and had obtained a license to drive a motorbike. I wanted to show off my skill at driving the bike and asked a hired hand, a field worker, if he would enjoy a bike ride with me one evening. "Yes," he said, "I never had a ride on a motorbike before." He was somewhat apprehensive climbing on the back seat, but did not want to miss out on some excitement.

I took the main road along the dike that overlooks the Zuider Zee, heading for the seventeenth-century seaport city of Enkhuizen. Electricity was still scarce and it was dark when we entered Enkhuizen.

Suddenly a shining red light appeared. I realized the local constable was checking incoming traffic. Since I did not have a motor vehicle document with me, I decided to evade him. First I slowed down. Then, as I made an abrupt turn into the side street, I gunned the engine, and then crossed a small canal bridge and turned off my headlights.

I could see the policeman trying to pursue me on his bicycle, without success as you can well imagine. My passenger on the back seat was somewhat scared, he told me later, but also felt the thrill of adventure.

Now what to do? I had few options. There were very few motorized vehicles right after the war. So it was very difficult to hide in a small city. It required subterfuge. Rather than making a long detour and risking meeting up with other policemen, I decided to circle around the city at low speed so as not to make much noise. Hopefully the policeman would still be searching in the other direction. Sure enough I got away without discovery and high-tailed it for home. My friend on the rear seat had the thrill of his life and had lots to talk about with his fellow workers.

A week later, still not having searched for the necessary motor vehicle operating papers, I went for another ride, this time in our own village. On my way home I spied our local policeman standing with his bicycle under one of the few streetlights, not far from our home. He waved his flashlight for me to stop. I thought, Once lucky, twice smart. How stupid can one get? The local cop knew everyone in our village who owned a motorcycle. As I roared passed him he followed me to our home. But, knowing he would stop at our home, I went on to my brother's place to see if he had the missing operating papers.

The police officer stopped at our home and gave my mother an earful. Meanwhile, at my brother's place a half-mile down the road, there was no sign of the motor vehicle papers; he neither had them nor could he tell me where they were.

I left to go home. Suddenly, red light was flashing and I knew I was in deep trouble. There was no use trying to evade him; there was another officer stationed behind me. I had no way out.

The local gendarme was very unhappy with me to say the least. His face went red as he cussed me out. He charged me with five offences and allowed me to go home. I had to appear the following day at the police station with the missing papers, he said, or be incarcerated.

I talked to my younger brother before facing my father to make my confession. My brother Gerrit told me the policeman had stormed into the house asking my mother where that darned son of hers was.

After a serious discussion, my dad counselled me on how to proceed with the charges against me: show your remorse and apologize profusely. I took his advice and faced the officer, who had cooled down considerably. I very meekly apologized, whereupon he dropped two of the charges, to save me from having to face a judge. I think he did it more for my father, whom he respected, than for me.

Lesson for the Day: Don't try to be a smart ass.

8

LEAVING HOME (1948)

In 1948, I was to be inducted into the Armed Forces of the Netherlands. One of my older brothers was already in military service and had been shipped to Dutch East India (also known as Indonesia), for active duty. His unit was on a mission to recover this colony of Holland, because the Japanese occupying forces had left. Some of the indigenous people were unhappy to see the Dutch return, no longer wanting a colonial presence. To thwart it, they started guerrilla warfare. Soon it would be my turn to be conscripted and to go, in my brother's footsteps, to Dutch East Asia.

While waiting for the call to duty, my two cousin friends, John Vriend and Peter Lieuwen, and I had been discussing our futures. We thought about what it would be like to emigrate to Canada, where we had relatives. I reasoned that, since I came from a family of twelve children and would always have a lot of competition for my parents' affection, my siblings wouldn't miss me. Moreover, I was considered the black sheep of the family.

My father was a very busy man. Managing his seed business took most of his time: contracting farmers to grow vegetable seeds, and handling, sorting, cleaning and repackaging seeds for shipment to retailers. He was also involved in volunteer work as a church elder and a village councilman. He often had to travel to meet with customers. This frequently left me under the supervision of my older brothers. As I was not yet very disciplined in my work habits, we occasionally clashed.

My father was extra patient with me, and he gained my respect. When I was younger, he would sometimes take me along on short business trips to keep me out of my mother's hair. If I did something requiring punishment he would get the "matten klopper" (carpet beater) and paddle my backside. Knowing his strictness but also his fairness, I could accept punishment when deserved. He was never harsh and would sometimes take me aside, discuss the problem and explain the consequences of the misbehaviour.

One time I again did something I knew was out of bounds and realized he would find out sooner or later. I felt guilty already. What was I to do? I thought the best approach was to go see him, tell him I did something wrong, apologize, hand him the carpet beater and offer my rear end, in my own version of reverse psychology. He was so impressed by my humble attitude that he just said, "I see you are sorry, we will let it go at that." I thought I saw an inner smile, through the twinkle in his eye.

I cannot say that I had a harsh or difficult life. My parents loved me. True, there was friction at times when my older siblings wanted to discipline me, but nothing beyond what is normal in families. On the whole we were a peaceful lot. So why would I leave this home, with all the comforts of life and a supportive family?

In one word: "ADVENTURE." We had just gone through a war and been liberated, mostly by the Canadian Army. We had relatives in Canada, and I was to be conscripted into the Dutch army. All these factors influenced my decision. Not that I feared a stint in the army; I actually wanted to experience those exotic places in Indonesia. However, it would delay our departure for Canada for at least two years. Therefore we three cousins, John, Pete and I, asked permission from our parents to emigrate to Canada. They approved, mostly because my father had visited Canada the year before and was impressed with its opportunities.

Decision made, we started dreaming of high adventure: sailing by steamship to Halifax, braving storms and high seas. Possibly we could obtain an army jeep in Halifax and drive across the country to our destination in British Columbia. No doubt we would meet up with wild Indians and cowboys. We talked of sleeping in the open air, foraging for food and fending off wolves (we had read fiction about that sort of thing in earlier years).

Needless to say, it was not exactly like that.

We three cousins left in April, 1948. We had bought dark blue berets and decorated them with the initials T. B. T. We thought of ourselves as "The Big Three", ready to conquer a new country. We boarded the "Kota Inten", an old troop ship lying in wait for us in the port of Rotterdam. Our departure was typical. As we sailed away, everybody on deck was screaming and waving, until out of sight, to their loved ones on shore. Everyone was cheerful. There was no inkling of the foul weather and discomfort which lay ahead.

The ship, which had previously been used to ferry soldiers to Indonesia, was now being used to transport immigrants to North America. Passengers slept in hammocks: men in the bow section of the ship where the rise and fall of the ship was greater, women and children in the stern. The hammocks were "stacked" three and four high. I took the top hammock, thinking that, if someone got seasick, he would not empty his stomach on my hammock or on me!

Once out of the English Channel and into the open waters of the Atlantic Ocean, the weather grew worse. On the third day, a storm came up. Waves came crashing onto the bow of the pitching ship. Great masses of spray would engulf the front of the ship making outdoor excursions impossible. Each time the ship came crashing down into a wave there was a thunderous sound, as if we had hit something solid. When the ship rode the crest of the wave the propellers at the stern would be exposed, allowing them to spin free with a great roar. Then the ship would shudder like a giant duck shedding water from his back.

Many passengers got seasick. Even quite a few of the stewards could not rouse themselves from their beds. When the captain asked for volunteers to help out, we three friends accepted the challenge. At first, we too felt somewhat nauseated, especially when sticking our heads into the food galley. We missed a few meals but soon got our sea legs. One of my duties was to help bring food and drink to the women and children in the rear section of the ship. I would hand out some plain bread and water and help the children get comfortable in their hammocks. Some women were too sick to get up and were grateful for the help, since their husbands were also sick in the front section of the ship.

I actually started to like the storm. Often, after finishing my chores, I would go to the upper deck and watch the waves wash over the bow. Every wave is different in height or appearance. Most headed straight for the bow, but now and then one would come from an angle, causing the ship to roll or wallow. After a few days the storm abated and we could all sit or walk around on deck.

While sitting on deck, studying the main mast with its cross beams and rigging, my mind got caught up in stories of sailing ships and exotic places. The thought came to me: what if I climbed the rope ladder to the first crossbeam to have a better look over the ocean? I mentioned the idea to my cousins, and they dared me to do it. So up I went on the rope ladder to the first cross beam, pausing to consider if I should go higher. Of course I was in plain view of the ship's bridge, and my cousins sent a crewmember to order me down.

After ten days of sailing we arrived in Halifax. Coming on shore there was no jeep waiting for "The Big Three". Instead, there was a special immigrant train of old coaches going rickety tick for six days to reach British Columbia. The train had overhead bunks against which I bumped my head on several occasions. We arrived safely, with no Indian raids or wolves to hinder our progress. I had fifty dollars when I boarded the train and thirty when I arrived at my destination.

9

MY NEW HOME IN CANADA (1948)

My cousins, Pete Lieuwen and John Vriend, and I had left the Netherlands to make Canada our new home. We traveled by boat to Halifax and, from there, rode the train west to British Columbia. It took five days to reach Edmonton, Alberta, partly due to our train being sidelined many times for more pressing traffic on the rails. We stopped in Edmonton for a few days to meet some friends of our parents. This gave us a respite from the long days on the train. From Edmonton to Houston, British Columbia, took another two days. We were welcomed at the railway station by several cousins whose families had settled there some years before (1939).

It was a bright sunny day in the month of May. My uncle, by whom I was to be employed, did not own an automobile. To pick us up at the train station, he had hitched a pair of horses to a farm wagon. We rode on the wagon with our baggage. This slow means of transportation gave us a chance to leisurely observe the countryside. In that short drive to our uncle's ranch—it was only a few miles—I remember crossing the Bulkley River, its banks overflowing with runoff from melting snow in the mountains.

I also remember the excited chatter of my cousins who had not seen us in ten years. And I noticed their clothes. Compared to ours they were more colourful, interesting. Our cousin Pete, for example, wore a red-

and blue-checkered shirt with baggy pants and a jaunty cap on his head. He had arrived from our home village only a year before, but his attire and manner of speech as he gave advice gave a feeling that he was a veteran already; he seemed fully acclimatized to his new Canadian surroundings.

When cousin Pete Lieuwen and I arrived in Houston (cousin John stayed behind to work for another cousin, Tom, in the Lacombe area), I stayed with my uncle Peter Ruiter, and Pete Lieuwen stayed with Herman Ruiter, an older cousin about 1/4 mile away.

My uncle's abode was an old ranch house constructed of pine logs. The exterior of the logs were weathered and cracked. To keep the cold air from entering, the slits between the logs were filled in with manure. The inside walls were covered with plaster boards. The kitchen contained a hand-operated pump which drew water from the well to the sink below the window. The well was hand dug, just outside the house. There was a mammoth cast iron, wood-burning stove. It had a reservoir to hold water and keep it warm for washing and bathing.

Bathing was a bit of an event. I used to strip to the waist in the kitchen to wash the upper part of my body. The bottom half got a turn only about once a week. This required me to carry a large basin of warm water up the stairs to my room for my Saturday wash. In winter, we would sometimes go to the home of a Swedish woman for a steam bath. She had a special cabin in her yard for this purpose. It had two small rooms: one to undress in, and one for the bath. The bath room had a fire-box made of a 45-gallon drum lying on its side with rocks were piled around it. When water was poured on the rocks, it created lots of steam. This hot steam would cause the pores of our skin to open and let out any impurities within. We had heard that the Finnish people, to cool off after such a bath, would roll in the snow. This physical masochism was supposed to harden the body. My friends and I could not adopt that idea and chose, instead, to pour cold water over our bodies to cool off.

The living room in my uncle's house was divided into two parts: the sitting room and the living and dining room area. The sitting room was seldom used and therefore not heated in the winter. It was separated from the other area by a wall with a large cut-out. In this "window" hung a heavy curtain to prevent cold from passing through. A heating stove was located in the living and dining room area, where we usually sat. This black, upright, cast iron, wood-burning stove was very ornate with its chrome handles and accents. Most of the furniture of the room was stout but comfortable enough, and there were a few easy chairs.

Since we had no electricity, the room was lit with a Coleman lantern using naphtha gas. Inside this glass-encased lantern was a sock-like bag called a mantle which, when lit, acted like a light bulb. Gas continued to squirt onto the mantle through pressure, fuelling the flame. This gave a flood of light, adequate for reading.

Reading was our main entertainment in the winter. Playing cards was not done, as my uncle felt such games related to gambling. The radio, which ran on batteries, was on a shelf behind the heavy curtain and was rarely used. My uncle admonished me once when I sought to tune it in for some lively music.

Since there was no indoor plumbing, we used the outhouse that was about 50 feet from the back door. Although, the fresh air helped combat the odour at any time of year, it was not a place in which one idled. It was bearable enough in summer temperatures, but in winter the outhouse was not a pleasant experience. Besides having to dress for the cold, you might have to remove wind-blown snow from the toilet seat. It was no place for a constipated person on a wintry day.

My uncle was a staunch Christian who practiced what he preached. He had a somewhat stern demeanour and a generally pessimistic disposition, but he could be humorous at times. Then I would roar with laughter, because I did not expect it from him. The following story gives a good example of this.

One day we were transferring hay from a wagon to the haystack, right beside the bull's corral. This bull had served a cow that morning and was now bellowing for dear life. My uncle suddenly blurted out, "What is the matter with you? Why don't you shut up? You just had the time of your life this morning, so now quit your complaining!"

When I met my uncle in 1948 he was 62 years old. He had moved there in 1939, at age 53. (I thought it was courageous of him to move at that age.) He spoke with a heavy accent but understood the language well, because he loved reading. He read a lot of novels, I remember, and I don't recall there being a library.

My aunt was a frugal homemaker. She would make fresh coffee in the morning and serve the warmed up leftover in the afternoon. My uncle once remarked, "Do you have any of that slough water left?" He just accepted it. I thought it tasted horrible, but I, too, did not complain. She was a typical homemaker of the times; meeting all her husband's needs: physical, mental and emotional. She did not, however, work in the field, probably due to her age.

My cousin Carolyn was the only child of five still at home. Carolyn was a quiet, unobtrusive 19-year-old. She was not active in the running of the farm either. After she finished helping her mother with the house chores each day, she went to her upstairs room and studied for her high school diploma. The local school only went to grade nine, so she had to prepare for college by correspondence lessons.

She was happy to see us male cousins. She had missed exposure to male friends, I surmised, because she was isolated from town and dependent on others for transportation.

We got along well. She was instrumental in teaching me the rudiments of the English language. She would ask questions, and I would try to answer in English. Then she would rephrase my response and make me repeat it.

My work experience on the ranch was a real treat. My uncle farmed only a square-mile section of land, some of it still original bush. One of my first work assignments was to plough a meadow, using three horses and a plough with a seat. I did not think of this as work. This was surely heaven: sitting on the plough instead of walking behind it. I said to myself, "Man, this is living!"

I liked working with horses. It was peaceful without the roar of tractors in your ears.

I could hear the horses' snorts and laboured breathing and could see their muscles rippling. I loved the sounds of leather harnesses creaking and the smell of horse sweat. The only smell that did not tickle my nose was that of horse gas.

I loved the outdoors. There were the sounds of birds flying by and the rich smell of the fields. I'd come across field mice, rabbits and sometimes a deer or a coyote. Even a bear could show up unexpectedly.

I remember one such unexpected visit on a day, later on, when I was trusted to use the tractor. It was a dusty day and, as I was driving along, I saw a figure in the distance. I thought it was my uncle coming to see how I was doing. It turned out to be a black bear, standing on its hind legs and watching me come in his direction. I stopped the tractor to unsheathe the knife from my belt in case I needed it. The bear, however, was not interested enough and soon took off, back into the bush. I guess he was just checking out the sound and smell of the machinery. When my heart stopped pounding, I resumed my work with the tractor.

Somewhat later I had another frightening close encounter with a bear. I was sent to fix a fence in a remote part of the ranch. I'd gone on foot and, when I finished fixing the break, I decided to return by way of a shortcut through the bush. I had only gone a short distance when a great noise came my way. Looking for its source, I saw a large moose come crashing through the brush. As it rushed past me, I looked to my left to see what scared this animal into such a hasty flight. There, under a large pine tree about a hundred feet from me, a big black bear sat on his haunches sniffing the air. I froze in my tracks, wondering whether he was in a defensive position or whether he was smelling the air for prey. One thing I knew: I had to get out of there! I dropped my tools, tiptoed a short distance, then ran the rest of the way back to the ranch as fast as I could. I arrived trembling and exhausted. It was my first close encounter with a bear. Later, I learned that they are just as afraid of humans as we are of them. If you stay out of their range of intolerance and make enough noise to make your presence known, they will go away.

I enjoyed working with my uncle. We milked a few cows in the morning, then fed the four horses and harnessed them for the day's work. Haying, although it was demanding in terms of strength and endurance, was one of my favourite tasks. Cutting the grass, by sitting on the mower with the horses pulling, was no hardship.

Haying was a relatively simple process. After cutting, the grass was left to dry in swaths for a few days. Then we would rake it together and heap it into small piles. After letting it cure for a few more days, we would load the hay onto the 'hayrack', a four-wheel wagon with wheels made of wood and rimmed with iron. On both ends of that flat wagon were two upright sections to keep the load of hay in place. The hayrack held about a ton of hay. A team of horses pulled it to the barn where it was unloaded with the help of a large fork. This two-pronged fork was stuck into the hay. A rope was attached to it and hauled over a pulley attached to the roof of the barn. The horses would pull the rope and the fork loaded with hay into the loft of the barn, then release it by pulling a smaller rope. It would take four lifts to empty the hayrack. After the hay was dumped we needed to spread it evenly over the hayloft.

As, I said, it was demanding work. Sometimes it was very hot in the hayloft, but I was young and strong and let the sweat pour down freely over face and body. My uncle, being over 60 years old, would let me do the heavy work. Loading the hayrack, I would pitch up the hay to him on the wagon and he would adjust the load. Once, when I pitched a heavy bundle of hay up to him, he remarked, "Francis, take it easy. You might not last the day." I chuckled to myself and drove the pitchfork even deeper into the pile of hay to show my strength.

The job of harvesting the grain—mostly oats and barley—was a more difficult task than the haying. We had a machine called a binder, pulled by four horses, which cut the grain, bundled it and wrapped twine around the bundle. The bundle was then dropped back onto the field behind the binder. Then the hard work started: stacking the bundles together in an upright position, 6 to 8 bundles to a stack. This way the grain kernels would dry and cure.

There were two things I hated: bundles that were wet from morning dew or rain, and being hit in the face by the tops of the bundles and having the fuzzy beard of the kernels stinging my face and skin. Such was the nature of farm work

What I liked best was to go horseback riding, playing cowboy on the range. After supper, it was my task to bring the cows in from their grazing on crown land adjacent to our farm. A few of the cattle wore cowbells for easy tracking, and the horse I was riding was trained to chase a wandering cow or steer. Once pointed in the direction of a stray cow, he would rush to the outside of the cow, forcing it to get back in line with the herd heading for the farmyard.

We did not have to milk the cows in the evening because we let the calves suck the mother's milk, but we separated a few calves from their mothers at night so we could milk those cows in the morning for domestic use.

There was a horse named Pete that was rather high strung and skilled in quick twists and turns. If you were not alert he could easily throw you out of the saddle. One time, I was out riding, inspecting a field of timothy grass and clover for noxious weeds and stopping now and then to get off the saddle to pull one. While I was moving along, slightly bent forward to see better, I saw a weed and called out, "Whoa!" Pete stopped alright, but he did it so fast that I slammed forward and mashed my testicles against the saddle horn. It was so painful I just slithered out of the saddle and lay on the ground catching my breath as the pain subsided. The horse looked down at me with bleak eyes as if he wanted to say, "You told me to stop!"

Such was my work and play on the farm in 1948. With harvest over and winter approaching there was little farm work left to do. It was time to find other employment in the forest industry.

10

THE FRUSTRATION
OF LANGUAGE

My mother tongue is Dutch, the language of the Netherlands. When I immigrated to Canada in April of 1948, I learned the English language by trial and error. Listening closely to others who seemed to know the English language, I imitated their speech, thinking to become proficient myself. I soon learned that not everyone I encountered spoke the language well and I had to discriminate between those who spoke in proper form and diction and those who did not. Many people I knew had a limited vocabulary and spoke with a foreign accent.

My first home in Canada was in northern British Columbia where my uncle and aunt and their children had immigrated to in the 1930's. The place is called Houston, which is situated about 180 miles west of Prince George.

At that time, it was a small town of about 500 inhabitants, approximately a mile and a half from the ranch my relatives owned. I worked for my uncle for the first two years and enjoyed the work in the field, especially haying and working with horses. I loved riding a saddle horse called Pete. He was a true cattle herder and it was my task to bring in the cattle from the outer parts of the ranch into the fenced in yard after supper.

The Buckley Valley where they lived was a very picturesque place, surrounded by hills and snow-covered mountains. The area was mostly covered in forest of spruce, pine, poplar and birch trees, with lots of wild life: moose, deer, wolf and coyote. I often heard the wolves howling in the distance.

As I was eager to learn the English language, I would read—or rather attempt to read—anything at hand: catalogues, newspapers, and, in particular, the Reader's Digest. I would read and reread until the words had meaning.

I practiced verbally with my cousin Carolyn. Whenever I had been out in the evening to attend a baseball game or some other entertainment I would relate my experience to her in English, and she, in turn, would rephrase my sentences in the proper form and make me repeat them. In this way, I became more proficient in proper form and pronunciation.

After two years of working, on the ranch in the summer and in lumber camps in the winter, my uncle suggested I try employment in other places and suggested I consider whether farming was truly my best option for a future career. He introduced me to some acquaintances in the Vancouver area. After writing to them, I was invited to come.

By this time I thought I was fairly competent in the English language. However, as I traveled by train to Prince Rupert and continued by boat{accidentally in first class) to Vancouver, I was exposed to people whose language and station in life I was not familiar with. I realized, then, that my vocabulary and fluency in English left much to be desired, except for some choice expletives perhaps, which I had learned in lumber camps.

Arriving in Vancouver in April of 1950, my first job was a ten-day stint with the owner of a large farm in Lulu Island, just across the Fraser River from the city of Vancouver. Although I lived in a dormitory with other farm hands, I felt a bit lonely and also lacked private transportation. I realized I needed wheels to get around and promptly went to a second-hand dealership where I bought a 1936 Buick Coupe with a straight eight engine. Boy, what a beauty! It cost every last dollar I had, $600.00.

Attending church the next Sunday with my new 'steed', I met a Canadian family of Dutch background who no longer spoke in their native tongue. They found me a job in a shingle factory, called Capilano Timber, situated along the Fraser River just outside New Westminster. Fortunately, the family who found me this employment offered me board and room as well, which I happily accepted. They were instrumental in improving my language skills. They also had a daughter my age, called Winny, who had her eye on me. Since I was not ready for matrimony, I decided, several months later, that it was time to move on. Besides, I did not think city life was for me. I started longing to be back in northern B.C. where my relatives and friends lived, amid the scenic landscape of the Bulkley Valley.

Two years later, in 1952, I moved to Edmonton where my sister Marie lived. Her husband, Henry, was a telegrapher and stationmaster for the Canadian National Railway. Henry convinced me that I should try that vocation as well. Although I could not see myself in an office environment, I thought the challenge intriguing and said to myself, "Why not?"

I had not anticipated the new frustration I experienced in having to learn the Morse code. The method of communicating via telegraph wires—in dots and dashes—was, in fact, a new language! I learned the telegraph code in my spare time. I remained employed at a nearby farm until after the harvest, and had time in the evenings to study. From there on, some friends took me in as a full-time student to train as a railway station attendant in Riley, Alberta's Canadian National Railway Station.

Oh! What anguish and frustration I experienced learning the Morse code! Numerous times I picked up my practice device, ready to throw it out the window. Only the inner voice kept me from doing so, and I would return to the practice set another day. I finally did pass my exam and was employed by the CNR in April of 1953 as a telegraph operator and assistant station agent. I worked there until January 1954. This experience helped me to improve my vocabulary and grammar skills and my ability to deal with the public.

With this experience I applied to, and was hired by, a seed company to represent them in retail sales during the winter and summer months. In late summer and fall I traveled throughout the Peace River countryside as a buyer of grass and clover seeds.

This experience as a buyer, in turn, prepared me for a position in sales. I became a life insurance agent and worked in that capacity for 30 years.

During these years, Prime Minister Trudeau was at the helm, and we were encouraged to become bilingual. Since I love to travel and visit foreign countries, I became intrigued. I took lessons and listened to tapes in the French language. I became somewhat proficient in French, enough to ask for directions and to order my food and wine. Subsequently, in 1979, I did travel with a backpack and a Euro-rail pass through France, Spain, Italy and Germany.

11

THE LUMBER JACK, PART I

Felling trees, skidding logs to loading areas, sawing logs into various sizes of planks and transporting them to planermills, were part of my experience in the years between 1948 and 1952. When farm labour was finished for the season, forestry was the only other employment. This was in Houston, B.C. where I lived with my uncle, Peter Ruiter. I worked on his farm for two summers and was employed at lumber mills during the winter.

In our first year there, Pete Lieuwen and I applied for winter jobs and were hired by H. Hagman's Sawmill about five miles from Uncle Pete's farm house. The roads to our bush camp were mostly just packed dirt, rough and sometimes deeply rutted. Bulldozers were used to cut through trees and brush, winding their way around obstacles and streams, up and along hillsides, gradually gaining height to where the sawmill was situated among heavy spruce and pine timber.

Our camp consisted of a cookhouse surrounded by the small cabins of the mill and bush workers. Our cabin was probably about 10' x 12', just big enough for two single beds with a small table between them and under the single window. We used sleeping bags on somewhat mouldy, smelly mattresses, with old pillows that most cats would avoid. There was an airtight, wood-burning heater; which we fuelled with dead wood or discarded lumber trimmings from the mill. The cabin walls were of 1" x 2" (2 ½ cm x 5 cm) lumber on 2" x 4" (5 cm x 10 cm) framing studs. The outside walls and roof were covered with tarpaper, but there was no insulation on the inside. Therefore, in below zero weather, in the absence of a fire inside the cabin, it would be just as cold inside as outside. To get a quick fire going we doused some diesel fuel on the wood. Since the cabins were small, they took only a short time to heat up.

In the morning, we did not bother to light a fire. We wore woollen long johns and would quickly slip into our clothes and head for the cookhouse for breakfast. After breakfast, we packed a lunch that was prepared and set out for us on the cookhouse table and walked up the hill about 800 yards to the saw mill. Work started at 8:00 am.

In those early days of the 1940's the saw mills were small and could be moved to where the trees were. It took about five men to operate a small mill. The foreman was usually the sawyer. His helper, the canter, would roll the log onto the carrier. The carrier moved past a large circular saw which cut or sliced the log into planks. The first cut off the log, the outer bark of the tree, was called a slab and would be waste. It fell onto a set of rollers and moved along to a worker called the "slab packer", who would carry it a short way and dump it on a burning pile. Slab packing was my first job. The next person to handle the lumber boards was the trimmer, who would cut the ends off each board to square it, and then cut it to its proper length: 12 or14 or16 feet. The trimmer would then give the board a push so it rolled on to the lumber packer, who would pile the lumber in 8 feet wide piles. Lumber packing was cousin Peter's first job. After packing, the boards would be hauled by lumber trucks, down the mountain roads to the planing mill in Houston. Our first experience as lumberjacks was quite an eye-opener. We had no idea how trees were cut, hauled and sawn into lumber.

The experience proved to be an ear-opener as well. In that first year (1948), the weather was still mild in October, so Pete and I would eat our lunch outside sitting on the lumber pile, while the rest of the crew would sit in the engine room where it was warmer. When the weather became colder, however, Pete and I joined the others. There, we were quickly initiated into very rough language. The men used unspeakable swear words that would redden our ears. We were still just learning the English language, not having had much practice with our Dutch-speaking relatives, but it wasn't long before we adopted some of those words ourselves. I remember one incident, a few months into the job, when a log fell on my toes and I let out a few choice expletives. I hadn't even known I could pronounce those words. I stood there quite perplexed and shocked at my own outburst! Yet, when I did not hear a disapproving thunderclap from above, I simply went on with my work.

Speaking of learning the language... It was my responsibility to clean sawdust from between the carrier tracks, but I did not know it. The foreman came over to me one day and asked, "Are you the farmer around here?" (This expression actually meant: Are you the boss around here?) Not understanding the expression, I nodded and said, "Yes." After all, I was from the farm! Then the foreman grabbed the shovel and cleaned away the sawdust, and I understood his meaning. But the foreman was not pleased.

On weekends we went to our respective homes. We would try to get a ride with a trucker carrying a load of lumber to Houston. We would ride on the top of the load since there was rarely room in the cab. In town we would spend a few hours visiting with friends, and shopping for sweets and tobacco, mostly at Koning's General Store.

Sometimes, on our way to the farm for the weekend, we would stop for a steam bath, or a "Finnish bath" as it was called. This steam bath was basically a cabin in which a steel drum lay on its side as a firebox, with rocks piled all around it. When water was splashed on the heated rocks it would create hot steam to clean our bodies. After sitting in the steam room for a while we would splash cool water over ourselves and feel cleansed. (We now know this as a sauna bath.)

On Sundays we attended church, twice, with our respective host families. It was not always interesting. We had no pastor for refreshing meditation, so church elders would read a sermons, mostly in accented English and sometimes in Dutch. However, it was still worship and fellowship. On Sunday evenings we went to Young People's Society meetings for some Bible study, singing and maybe a game. This was also an opportunity to meet girls, that is, possible future dates.

By 9:00 p.m. we would be back on our way to bush camp, stopping at our uncle's farm to change back to work clothes and have some hot chocolate and cake. From town to the farm was about 2 km; from the farm to the camp, another 8 km. There was no other traffic going our way on Sunday evenings.

It was very dark when the sky was cloudy, but most times the moon and stars were out to light the way. Sometimes it would be brutally cold: -30° C. We stayed warm by walking and by wearing wool clothing and heavy parkas. We often heard wolves howl in the distance, but we were not afraid. Only one time were we a bit scared when a large herd of moose came nibbling on trees and brush. This was in an area where, years ago, a forest fire had burned the trees, and new growth was sticking out through the snow.

We would arrive at our camp close to midnight, make a quick fire and crawl into our sleeping bags. There would be only six hours left before the morning gong sounded for breakfast. The meals were always very good: bacon and eggs, sometimes a pork chop. At dinner there was always a lot of meat, potatoes and canned vegetables.

The other bush workers were from various backgrounds. A few of them were Indians (indigenous people). Some were farmers who worked for extra income. Others were well-educated men that had been employed professionally but became alcoholics and needed to stay away from town and temptation. Still others were drifters, living full time in the camp to make quick money and move on. Finally, there were the permanent, professional lumberjacks.

Towards spring, I got fired by the owner of the sawmill, Mr. Hagman. I had talked back to him after he gave me advice on a method of work. He said nothing at the time, he just showed up the following week with a replacement worker. This ended my first winter in the bush, and I spent the summer of 1949 on my uncle's farm again.

12

THE LUMBER JACK, PART II

In the fall of 1949, Pete Dieleman was building a more modern saw-mill than Hageman's about 15 miles southeast of Houston, B.C. I asked to be employed there that October.

Harvest was finished early that year and I looked forward to leaving my uncle's farm for some new adventure. That is exactly what I got. My first assignment was to bring two horses from Houston up to the lumber mill camp. These two horses had been roaming free for the summer on an uninhabited ranch and on crown land west of Houston. They were lassoed by cowboys and left in Houston to be transported to the bush camp and used as skid horses.

I was used to working with horses and thought bringing them to the bush camp would be a piece of cake. They appeared tame enough. One horse was quite big and heavy, a real draft horse and easy to lead. I considered myself a competent horseman and felt the best approach would be to ride the fat one bareback and lead the other by a rope on his halter. In fact, I would attach the rope to my horse's halter ring. The second horse, however, was more spirited than the first and had a temperament not unlike my own: "Don't tell me where to go." Both horses had been free all summer and were not in the mood to be put back to work.

All went well for a mile or so. I was riding high on the horse's back and humming a song, "O what a beautiful morning! O what a beautiful day…" Suddenly, the more frisky horse sensed he was going in the wrong direction, away from his former range, and stopped. No urging helped; he would not move on. I got off my horse and thought that, if I walked ahead holding on to the rope, they would follow. They didn't. At this point, we still had more than 10 miles to go. I tried subterfuge. Turning them around, I backtracked a few yards, then turned around again. They would go for a bit, then stop again. I used my trick several times, but they were getting smarter. I needed to do something different.

I had no bridle for the other horse. Otherwise, I would have ridden him and slammed my heels into his sides to make him move. Just when I thought I had a solution—to tie him closer to the other horse's halter—the rope slipped out of my hand and the frisky horse took off, trotting in the other direction. Quickly, I jumped on the fat horse and pursued him. It didn't take much to see that this was futile; the clumsy draught horse was no runner. It seemed hopeless. Just then a car came our way. The driver saw the situation and stopped, parking at an angle on the road. He got out, spread his arms wide and was able to grab the rope dangling from the halter. I was greatly relieved. I'd had visions of pursuing that horse for ten miles or more.

After tying the two horses together I cut a branch from a nearby tree. I had enough rope that I could walk closely behind them. By dangling the branch with its rustling leaves over their backsides I kept them at a brisk walk. We stopped at a river crossing and I let them drink. After that, we still had five miles to go. We arrived at the bush camp six hours after leaving Houston. I stabled the horses and, even though I didn't think they deserved it, gave them some hay. I was grateful to have arrived, despite my sore rear and stiff legs. The fellows at camp laughed and joked about my ordeal, but I knew I had earned their respect by getting the job done.

I was not asked to go to work with these horses right away. There were other things to be done first. The new sawmill had been built in the middle of a virgin forest and the site was not quite ready. The trees around the mill had to be cut first. I was assigned to help the man who felled the trees.

To fell a tree requires some talent. First you have to decide in which direction the tree should fall: downhill, for example. If a tree is leaning too much in the other direction, obstacles need to be taken into consideration, such as other trees. Next, you make a small horizontal cut, about

15 cm deep, into the base of the tree on the side facing the direction in which you intend it to fall. Then, with an axe, a piece is chopped out just above the cut, on a sharp diagonal. This will prompt the tree to fall and create a clean break from the stump. When sawing into the tree, if the tree is leaning a degree or two away from the intended direction, the feller will hammer steel wedges into the cut to force it in the right direction.

Some of the trees in the area were as big as 4 feet (1.2 m) in diameter and 75 feet (22 m) tall. This required a two-man chain saw, which had a longer blade than the smaller one-man saw. This power saw has a gas engine, which drives a chain of sharp edged knives. The tree feller holds the heavier side of the chainsaw and controls the speed and tilt. The helper stands on the other side, holding onto the handle attached to the blade.

The tree faller was in charge around the mill, and, for this task, I was the helper assigned to him. I had no previous experience and wasn't given any instruction beforehand. New workers like me simply watched and learned on the job. The helper is supposed to stand in a position in extension of the blade, not behind the blade, as I did on this occasion. Standing behind the blade, I pulled it towards me, not moving backwards. The chainsaw cut through the tree as expected, but also through my coveralls, pants, and long johns just above my knee. Maybe a few hairs were cut, but the blade didn't break the skin. The operator, looking my way and seeing what was happening, hollered and stopped the engine, expecting blood to come spurting out. Fortunately, I was not hurt, but I was shocked and frightened enough that I quit for the day. So much for the introduction to handling a chain saw. Some days later I was put to skidding logs.

To skid logs we used a single horse, skidding the logs on narrow trails between stumps and trees that had been left standing. We used a steel hook, a half-circle pincher device, to grab the log. When attached to a chain pulled by a horse, the hook would bite into the log. The logs were hauled to a loading area to be trucked to the mill site.

I had chosen the frisky horse for skidding for two reasons: one, he matched my temperament in needing to get a move on and, two, I wanted to get even and show him who was boss. I worked him for the few weeks it took to get the sawmill site ready. The horse gave me no problems; we had mutual respect and were at peace with each other.

I was recruited by Dieleman's foreman, Joe Mulder, to work in the mill and be trained as an edger operator. The edger was the second set of saws after the main saw had sliced the tree into planks. I would estimate by eye the width of the plank, then set the saws with their long handles to the proper widths. The plank had to be pushed gently into the edger saw, which would cut the bark off either side and create a suitable width of 10, 15, 20, 25 or 30 cm. The next man would trim the ends, and someone else would pile the lumber for transport. The waste would fall on a conveyor belt and be dumped into the fire pit.

I enjoyed this work and was good at it. I had a sharp eye for getting the most out of a rough-cut plank, not wasting any more than necessary. I got along well with the foreman who later trained me to operate the main saw.

Again we lived in cabins with no insulation. We needed to keep the heater going. When the temperature got lower than -30°C, we could not work because of the danger that saw teeth might break loose and other metal equipment might crack. Often, during the night, the water in the cabin would freeze over.

One time after a weekend absence, I came to camp on a Sunday evening by myself when it was -40° C. It was scary, being alone in the dark and bitterly cold. I had to stop and think what to do first. I had to be careful not to touch any metal with bare hands; it could take the skin off the fingers. The lantern was too cold to handle, so I needed to make a fire first. Using a stick of wood, I lifted the lid of the stove, threw in some wood and splashed diesel fuel on it. Next, I took my mitten off, lit a piece of paper with a match and threw it into the stove. Lifting the lantern with a stick of wood, I put it on the stove for a little while until I could use my bare hands to lift and light it. I knew that one mistake could cost me my life. I could freeze. Or I could have an accident lighting a fire.

In the spring of 1950, I moved to Vancouver to see what that city had to offer.

13

MY FIRST SET OF WHEELS

I arrived in Vancouver from Houston B.C in the early spring of 1950. I found employment as a farm hand on Sea Island, presently the site of the Vancouver International Airport. I was one of about five farmhands living in an upstairs bunkhouse, above the kitchen and eating area, and the farmer's office.

The only way I could get from the farm to the city proper was by catching a bus—and buses ran infrequently—or by getting a ride. I needed transportation badly. So, I decided to get a car from second-hand car lot I had seen somewhere in the middle of town. When I first approached a salesperson called George, I said that I was interested in a secondhand car, preferably a coupe. He did not have one on the sales lot, but he promised that he would find one for me and phone me.

Sure enough, a week later, George left a message for me to come and see what he had found. It was a 1936 Buick coupe. It had a straight eight engine and one bench-style seat which could accommodate three people comfortably. It had a large elongated trunk. It looked quite attractive with its large, round headlights affixed to the two front fenders. I looked over this shiny car with its leather seats and at the powerful engine under the hood. "What do you think, Francis?" said George, "Isn't it a beauty?" I was drooling.

Over the two previous years, working as a farmhand and a bush-whacker, I had saved up about $600. I must have mentioned something to the salesman about my approximate savings because $600.00 was exactly the price he quoted! Since I was a greenhorn in dealing with a car salesman, I took his word for it. I didn't know about bargaining. I had withdrawn almost all my savings from the bank the day before, and now I just handed over the money. However, when the salesman became aware that I'd given him pretty well the last dollar I possessed, he refunded me two dollars for fuel to put in the near-empty tank.

I had had experience in driving a car before coming to Vancouver but was not eligible for a driver's license, because I had not reached my 21st birthday. Since I did not have a license, the salesman suggested I take a circuitous route home to avoid police surveillance. So, off I went, bought some fuel and made it safely back to the farm.

I named the car Lucille. Proud as a peacock, I took my Lucille to the next Young People's Society meeting. Here my new acquisition was admired and, to my great surprise, right after our meeting three girls piled into the front seat! There wasn't quite enough room for everyone, but we all squeezed in. We had the time of our life riding in Lucille. The girls were ecstatic, saying what a beautiful car it was and how lucky I was. I wondered, Did I suddenly become popular? Well, maybe somewhat, but it was more the novelty; cruising around the city and going to a park and a beach was exciting. It was a bit crammed with four of us in the front seat, but manageable. I drove the girls home. The last one was slow to leave the front seat, wanting to make more conversation, but my mind was elsewhere. My newly acquired automobile was my first love.

A few weeks later, when I turned 21, I decided it was time to obtain my driver's license. The week before, I had had quite a scare. I had come to a large intersection—I think it was Centre Street and Kingsway—and I had to make a left turn. As there were no traffic lights, a policeman was directing traffic. I was somewhat unsure about his signals, and the traffic gendarme was waving a finger at me, as if to say I should know the rules. A close call, I thought. Luckily, I was not asked to pull over for inspection and show a license.

Arriving at the licensing bureau a few days later, I picked up an application, together with a small booklet to study the rules of the road. Choosing a desk a distance from the front counter, I started reading the information and filling it in on the form. Nobody took notice of me, and I thought, That is kind of neat, I don't need to take the booklet home to study. So, after finishing the form, I handed over the application and set a date for the driver's test. I completed it a week later without a problem.

In the meantime, I had met a family at church who very kindly took me to their home since I was new and, no doubt, a bit lonely. I had let it be known that I was not happy with my present employment. This resulted in my host, Mr. Hiemstra, introducing me to his place of work, a shingle factory situated along the Fraser River. He also offered me room and board with them. A few days later, I got a phone call that the factory would hire me, pronto. After finishing my day's work on the farm, I drove to the factory and started working on the night shift, till midnight. I was totally worn out by the time I reached the farm's bunkhouse that night. The next morning I gave my notice to the farmer.

I was very fortunate. I had better employment, at $1.15 per hour. I had been taken in by a really nice family, and I had a nice car, the Buick coupe. It was a great new start in the summer of 1950. In reciprocation to my benefactors, I gave them rides whenever I had the opportunity.

By the end of the summer, I decided to return to Houston. It was a 700-mile drive northward, along the beautiful Fraser River. I stopped overnight in Prince George, freeing Lucille of the dust from the gravel roads. The next day, my cousins welcomed me back, and I proudly showed them my shiny Buick with its straight eight engine. I demonstrated how powerful it was by driving up the fairly steep incline of "Hungry Hill" and not having to gear down.

The roads in some places in northern British Columbia were wicked in terms of rocks and bends. Once, on a very rough section, coming around a bend, the vibration from the rocky surface caused the passenger door to come undone. My cousin Bill, sitting next to the door, held on to the seat (there were no seatbelts in those days) and held his breath. Then we both laughed, thinking it funny. But it was not funny; he could have fallen out and been seriously injured or could have lost his life. Some angel must have been there, shaking his or her head.

On another occasion, I took a coworker named Fred along to Telkwa, some 40 miles' distance from Houston, where we had a few beers. Driving home, just before dusk, the headlights would not come on. I kept driving, wanting to make time before full darkness set in. We did not make it. I had to follow someone ahead of me, watching his taillights until we arrived at our destination. Fred bragged to his friends about our journey in the dark and it became the talk of town, this daring drive in darkness.

By the time winter arrived, my Lucille had traveled over quite a few rough roads. She required an overhaul, and it would be expensive. She needed new tires and a wheel alignment. Also, the exhaust was spouting blue smoke. I parked Lucille in my uncle's farmyard, considering what to do. A few days later winter set in. The radiator froze and blew a few gaskets. I didn't have money for the repair. I left Lucille looking very tearful with her drooping headlights that had come loose from their bearings on the front bumpers.

Employed in Dieleman's lumber camp, deep in the woods, that winter, I managed to save a few dollars. In the spring I decided to part with Lucille and bought a new 1951 Ford pickup truck. It was more rugged and suitable for rough roads, especially the sometimes bumpy and muddy bush roads.

I missed my sexy Lucille but she left me with great memories. Life went on and I adjusted to the new reality of the day with the half-ton pickup truck.

14

TAXI DRIVER
(and the definition of "having fun")

In February of 1953 I had been unemployed for several months and was running out of money. I searched all over Edmonton for work, but nothing turned up that suited my disposition.

I was boarding with my married sister, who already had several children to support and I did not want to be a burden to her. I had spent my last dollars watching movies; a matinee theatre ticket cost 25 cents and I often managed two movies in an afternoon.

As I got to know the city a little bit better, I thought maybe I could become a taxi driver until a better opportunity came up. I had a Class A driver's license, obtained for driving a truck some years earlier. Although I had not lived in Edmonton very long, I had become familiar with the system of numerically listed streets and avenues. I had also spent some time riding buses around the city. I figured it could not be too difficult to be a taxi driver.

I applied for the position of chauffeur with a well-known taxi firm. They asked if I had a driver's license. I showed them my first class license. Next they asked if I knew the city and its street system and I told them yes. They suggested I ride along with an experienced taxi driver and come back for an answer.

The next day I rode along with my supposedly experienced instructor and presented myself as a very knowledgeable person with good manners, always getting out of the taxi and opening doors for our customers. He tried to trick me by asking me if I knew a particular road called "Power Road," a short side road off Kingsway Avenue. By chance I did know it. I had been there the week before. My experienced taxi driver was impressed and recommended me highly for the position of taxi driver or chauffer or Taxi driver. I was to report the following day for duty.

Arriving for duty at 8 am the next day, I had just settled into my appointed vehicle when the dispatcher called me on the radio and asked me to proceed to an address near our office. I found it readily enough, but I was still a bit nervous. My first customer was a man with his pregnant wife. They needed to go to the Misericordia Hospital. It did not bode well for me that I did not know where the hospital was located. I knew about the hospital but only its approximate location. Dwelling on that problem while driving and coming to the first stoplights, I stepped on the brakes too hard and heard a groan in the back seat. "Sorry, Ma'am," I stammered, "the light changed unexpectedly." Phew!

Getting closer to the hospital, I asked for a more exact location. It was given without any contempt towards me for being an inexperienced taxi driver.

During the following days, I continued to manage okay and was assigned to a more delicate part of Edmonton. I was to park in front of hotels on 96th Street, between 101st Avenue and 103rd Avenue. I was getting customers who wanted transportation to another hotel three to four blocks away. I wondered why they did not walk.

On another occasion, a few rowdy men needed transportation to a liquor store several miles away. Their language burned my ears.

Then there was a personal call for taxi number 29. It was a woman who needed transportation from a downtown hotel to her home in north Edmonton. I wondered what that meant: "taxi #29". How did she know me? I learned later that the former driver of my vehicle had had a business on the side.

As I drove to this woman's home she talked about a sailor who was a greenhorn with women. I did not make the connection to her profession at first, but it came to me when she paid for the taxi ride and out fell a condom. I was the greenhorn I realized, but I was learning fast.

On another occasion a girl of about eighteen requested taxi # 29. She was pretty and asked to be driven to a spot about four blocks away. She started to make conversation, giggled a bit and then made a proposition to go somewhere and have some fun. I declined the offer. My hormones had not yet been educated in what it meant to "have fun". They did act as a battle group, however, waiting for orders. By never having given any, I had kept them rudderless, you might say, which is what helped me to decline the girl's invitation. I must admit, though, that the prospect of having fun did linger in my mind for several days.

Fortunately, my employment as a taxi driver was short-lived. I received a call to come for an interview for the position of telegraph operator for the CNR and was hired after passing a test in Morse code.

15

CHRISTMAS IN BED
(1953)

It was a blistery day on Christmas Eve in the small town of Camrose, Alberta. I was 23 years old and single, walking toward the Canadian National Railway station where I was employed as an agent's assistant. Having the weekend off, I decided to check the train schedule, hoping to hitch a ride on a freight train to Deville some hundred miles away.

I had had a tired feeling that morning. Now, as I walked the four blocks from my boarding house, a cold wind penetrated my windbreaker.

Arriving at the railway station the manager in charge wanted to know why I was showing up on a day off. "Sorry, Sir," I said, "I wanted to see if there was a chance to hitch a ride on a train headed for Deville", and I explained my dilemma. A certain Morrow family near Deville had employed me as a farm labourer the previous summer and had invited me for Christmas, before I took the position in Camrose. The Morrow family had been very kind to me, providing me with room and board as well as my pay. I wanted to accept their invitation, but had no means of transportation, other than walking.

The second reason for wanting to celebrate Christmas with that family was an attractive daughter, Lillian, who was also to be there for Christmas.

Alas! There were no indications that a train would be coming along. Disappointed and cold, I noticed that my throat felt raw and decided to head back to my boarding place. To my dismay, the rooming house was totally deserted when I arrived. Not even the hostess was there to greet me. I trudged upstairs to my room, crawled into bed and lay shivering through the night, feeling very sad. I awoke Christmas day, still feeling feverish. I slid out of bed and went downstairs to see if there was anything to nibble on.

Finding no food to titillate my low appetite, I dragged myself back upstairs into bed, feeling lonely. I wished I had some medication to relieve my fever. By noon I decided to contact a doctor who was on duty.

The doctor arrived shortly thereafter. I met him in the downstairs hallway and he checked me over with his scope right on the spot. He concluded that I had strep throat. Producing a needle of penicillin, he told me to drop my pants and stuck the needle into my buttock, forcing the medication under the skin. While buttoning my pants, the sad expression on my face would have impressed a priest at confession. The doctor read it plainly, "It is Christmas and I am lonely, lonely, lonely." Unfortunately, he explained, my condition was still infectious and it would not be wise for him to invite me to his home. When the doctor left, I dragged myself back to bed once more and buried my self-pity in the pillows.

I awakened the following morning to find that the fever had left me. I dressed and went downstairs. My landlady, Ms. Proudfoot, finally returned home around lunch time. Her eyes widened when she saw me. "Merry Christmas!" she managed. After I explained my ordeal, she expressed pity, then straightened quickly when she realized I needed some food! Taking immediate action, she produced a delayed Christmas dinner for me which I greatly relished.

Comforted by the delicious meal, I was renewed both in energy and in my outlook on life. I promised myself I would look up the Morrow family at a future date. I looked forward to sharing with them my Christmas experience in Camrose as well as my work experiences with the Canadian National Railway.

16

GRAND PRAIRIE, AB
(OCTOBER 1955)

Dear Grace,

I am so sorry about not being able to see you this weekend. The rain is so bad, the roads are almost impassable. There is no way to travel by car or truck.

I miss you so much. I always feel so comfortable talking to you, as if I am at home with my own family—knowing and understanding each other, having a similar background, nothing to hide in our past, just feeling free and wanting to be together and hoping some day to be able to get together every day.

Living in a hotel for weeks on end gets so dull when rain prevents you from traveling and visiting farmers to discuss the value of their harvest. About the only thing that you can do is go to the bar for a beer, but you can only take in so much of that before it becomes boring.

The days here, buying grass and clover seed for Steele Briggs Seeds will end when the snow comes down in a week or two. Then I will be stationed in Edmonton maybe until next summer.

Again, Grace, may I call you sweetheart? I am feeling so in love with you. I intend to buy a ring for you and hope and pray you will accept it.

Looking forward seeing you next week. In the meantime...

An ocean of love and on every wave a kiss.

17

GETTING MARRIED

It was November 1955. Fall weather had set in, and I had just returned from traveling to the Peace River area where I had bought grass and clover seeds. I was about to begin a regular working routine in the retail warehouse of "Steel Briggs Seeds".

My Parents had come from Holland that June and were visiting me and my sister Marie. One Sunday, I suggested we attend a church service in Beverly since the pastor there, a new arrival from Holland, would probably preach in Dutch.

After the service, socializing on the patio outside the church, we talked with some friends we knew when a woman stepped up to my dad and said, "Hi, Uncle Gerrit." I was perplexed. Who was this woman who knew my dad but was unknown to me?

Her name was Grace, and it was explained to me that her grandfather and my step-grandfather were brothers. Therefore, there was no blood relation. Grace had arrived from Holland a few months earlier and had come to church with her brother John and his wife Jane. John had lived in our village of Andijk for a few years during the war.

John and Jane invited my parents and me to their home to get reacquainted. While my mom and dad where having coffee with their hosts in the living room, my interest was in the young woman. "Why don't we sit outside and talk?" I asked. She promptly agreed. Her features and easy conversation impressed me. At some point she mentioned that she had to take a bus way out to the west end of the city where she was employed as a nanny. I suggested giving her a ride, which she accepted. Of course I asked if we could meet again. Luckily for me she said, "Sure" and gave me the phone number of her employers' home.

Our first date was on the first of July. Together with another couple, we went to Victoria Park where we enjoyed the sun and shared our backgrounds and interests. I had no vehicle of my own at the time, but a kind friend gave us a ride there and back. Of course I set up another date.

Our friendship grew easily and quickly. We enjoyed discovering each other's tastes and learning about the things we had in common. We recognized our common heritage and our common beliefs; the values we shared concerning church and life.

In August, unfortunately, I was sent to the Peace River area as a buyer of clover and grass seeds and was stationed in Grand Prairie in a hotel. For a while, I was able to get home for most weekends and I always made sure that Grace and I spent a large part of at least one day together. However, when October came around, we had a lot of rain and bad roads. One weekend, after it had rained for several days, I was stuck in a small hotel in a little village called De-bolt about 50 km south of Grand Prairie. I felt bored and lonely and wrote a letter to Grace explaining that I was prevented from coming to Edmonton. It was a love letter about missing her and that I was thinking about buying a ring for her and hoped she would accept it. It was the first time I used the word "sweetheart".

I knew Grace was right for me. She was familiar with the type of work I was doing. When we were together there was an intimate atmosphere, a feeling of complete trust in each other. She had a happy countenance, a ready smile. As a bonus, she was healthy with a slim figure and an elegant bearing.

By the end of October, when the first snow fell, I was called to finish up my work and come back to Edmonton. I looked forward to getting together with Gre (as she was named in Dutch) as soon as possible. In the beginning of November, I obtained use of the company car, picked her up and took her to a restaurant for coffee and apple pie. (In those days, making a dollar an hour, I did not think about going for dinner.) Finishing our coffee and tasty pie, we gazed at each other with longing and desire to be together for the rest of our lives. Then I presented her with the ring I had bought and, without any hesitation, I put it on her finger. She smiled with a quiver of her lips and we kissed without any concern about being watched. Right there and then we began discussing wedding details.

We went to John and Jane's and informed them of our plans to get married in December. (I was not going to wait; we were in our mid twenties and sufficiently mature, so there didn't seem to be any need to wait longer.) However, John said, "Hold on. I am traveling to Holland in December and won't be back till January." I did not like it and would rather have married without him than wait. But Grace said, "It's all right, Francis, we can stick it out till February and set a date for February seventeenth, just 3 days after Valentine's Day."

In the meantime, we had time to find a place to live. We looked for a place to rent but were not excited about what we saw. Then John suggested a home that had just been built across the street from them. It did not have a cement floor in the basement and it did not have running water. Water pipes from the village had not yet been laid in that street, and it might be another year before water was available. But the price was reasonable: $9500.00 with $1500.00 down and five percent interest on the remaining mortgage. Although I was making $48 a week when we got married, it still scared me somewhat. But we made the deal. I bought a couch with a matching armchair, a small coffee table and a double bed with one chair. For the kitchen, we bought a natural gas stove. Including the down payment, we spent about $2300 dollars.

I had saved about $2500 over the previous two years, mostly through my traveling job, living in hotels and banking the rest of my weekly wages. At times, I had been tempted to buy a new car for that money but resisted, thinking to myself that I might run into a woman I'd fall in love with and need those savings. I thanked God for leading me in this.

The house was about 1000 square feet on the main floor, divided into five rooms: the bedroom, the living room, the spare bedroom, the kitchen and the bathroom. The bathroom, although complete with a tub and toilet, had no running water. Therefore it was of little use until it was connected with the town's water system. Meanwhile, water was delivered by a tank truck and funnelled through a window into barrels in the basement once a week.

The day of our wedding went well and was a very emotional day for us. Our brothers and sisters were excited, too. They had helped with many practical arrangements as well as advice.

Grace had not been able to save much money from the $50-a-month income she had earned in the seven months before our marriage. A friend named Mary lent Grace her wedding dress. Before we drove to the church, my sister-in-law Jane called me into the girls' dressing room to view the bride. I was astounded and almost in tears when I laid my eyes on her. In my eyes, she was a princess I could not have dreamed of. Jane had the right idea in letting me see her before the wedding started, so I would not be too emotional while making our wedding vows in front of the pastor and guests.

The wedding ceremony went well, attended by a few family members and friends plus about half of our church congregation.

Pastor Knoppers led the ceremony, which ended with a beautiful a cappella solo of the Lord's Prayer by my brother-in-law Henry Uitvlugt. The pastor, who was new to the Canadian way of allowing the bridal couple to kiss after completing the vows and omitted it, made up for it afterwards with a short speech during the reception. I believe we were the first couple he married after emigrating from Holland in June 1955.

The reception was held in the basement of our church. All the invited quests gathered for refreshments and a cold buffet. I had made arrangements with the concierge and his wife to hire a few teenage girls to do the serving. Several of the guests made a short speech or presented a poem or acted out a comical skit depicting something of our past. It was a beautiful evening. The total cost of the wedding was about $150.

At about 11 pm we were driven to our newly acquired home. According to tradition, I lifted Grace in my arms and carried her over the threshold into our modest castle. To us newlyweds, it was a castle.

We lived there peacefully for 6 years. After that we lived in Calgary for 3 years before returning to Edmonton, where we have lived for the past 43 years. This past month (February 2008) we celebrated 52 years of marriage.

18

THE FAMILY EXPANDS

Grace had taken on domestic work in the home of a nearby family in the first few months of our marriage, and we always had breakfast together before boarding the bus for work. Some time in the second month of our marriage, Grace seemed to lose her morning appetite. She wondered if she had the flu. When she hadn't recovered after a few weeks, she consulted her sister-in-law Jane. Jane smiled and asked a few more questions. Still smiling, she said, "I think you should go to the doctor; you might be pregnant."

"Not already!" Grace gasped.

Well, after taking a urine sample, the doctor confirmed the pregnancy and informed Grace that the baby was due "exactly 9 months and two days from your wedding day".

"Close call!" said Grace, "I'm glad it is a day or two later; our neighbours, friends and church family can count on their fingers to check the days and conclude that all is in order."

The baby did arrive right on the date the doctor had given. Saved from wagging fingers!

We named our first-born Linda, a somewhat convoluted form of my mother's name, Alida. We were very thankful to receive a healthy child. Of course, it still took a lot of attention in the first year. Grace was a very good caregiver and managed well.

During her early pregnancy however there had been a mood change. Grace's husband did not always understand why, and it caused a bit of friction now and then. Grace, being a perfectionist, would criticize her husband when he did not follow her instructions of closing cabinet doors right away after use. On a particular time he did not like to be criticized and let out an expletive. It shocked her; never had she heard this before! "That is a terrible swear word," she said, "Are you not ashamed."

"Yes, but don't bug me about nonsensical things!"

After Linda was born, Grace's parents came from Holland to visit us and stayed for a large part of that year. By then, Grace found herself pregnant again and was happy to have her mother to help a bit around the house. A year later, two days before Linda's first birthday, our second daughter was born. We named her Carolyn after one of my sisters. She weighed less than her sister Linda and was a little more delicate. I guess we should have been more careful in timing the cycle of fertility to prevent having a second child so soon. In those days we were ignorant about contraceptives; it was definitely not the talk of the day.

Carolyn needed more attention, wanting to be fed every three hours or so. Breastfeeding on demand, day and night, was a hardship for Grace. I could not help her there.

When Carolyn was a bit older, Grace added a little pabulum to the diet. It consisted of a very fine ground meal dissolved in milk. On one particular occasion, when baby's mother had to go out for the evening, I, her smart father, had to feed her. I had been instructed as to how much pabulum powder I should mix with the milk. I thought I'd enhance baby's mixture so that Mother would not have to feed her every three hours. I added a little extra powder to the milk. It did not take long for little Carolyn to throw up her food due to its indigestible thickness. Of course I was rightly rebuked when mother hen came home. I had no defence and had to accept the chastisement.

With Grandma Vriend available to help Grace (Granddad Vriend helped his son John in his landscaping business) all went well for the next 6 years.

After that, I was transferred from Edmonton to Calgary as a life insurance agent. We lived there for three years. We rented a home in the first year, then bought one.

Our third daughter, Marianne, was born there in 1963. She was a doll of a preschooler, happily walking around the house following her mother, sometimes standing by the window overlooking the street and watching passers-by, or playing with the doggie called Co-co next door in the neighbours' backyard. The first word she was taught to say was "Daddy". It was my turn, Grace said, to get up in the middle of the night when she called. It worked; I would get up when she called "Daddy" and would stroke her head or back until she went back to sleep.

It was back in Edmonton that Linda went to school for grade one, not far from our home. We taught her the route from home to school and back by walking with her a couple of times. The first day of walking by herself, she panicked and rang a doorbell about half-way there. A woman phoned us, and Grace picked up a teary-eyed daughter. In Edmonton, in September 1964, there was no worry about kidnapping (or vandalism or other street behaviour). The school was nearby, an easy walk for the two oldest girls.

When Marianne started going to Kindergarten, she walked with her sisters to school in the morning. Because she was dismissed a half hour earlier than the others, Grace picked her up at the end of the day. On one particular day, when Grace came to pick her up, Marianne asked her mother, "If Jesus came back and you are not home, could I take my stuffed animal Co-co* along?" (*named after the doggy that she used to play with next door in Calgary)

We lived in that Edmonton neighbourhood, called McQueen, for twelve years. In 1976, we moved to "Westridge", where we lived for thirteen years. From 1989—1996 we lived in "Country Club", and from 1996-2005 in "Terra Losa". Our most recent move—and maybe our last—was in September 2005, to a beautiful seniors' centre named Touchmark.

19

SELLING LIFE INSURANCE

One sunny summer day in 1958 someone knocked on our door and introduced himself as Klaas Terpstra. He was the branch manager of the Holland Life Insurance Company in Edmonton. His objective was to recruit me as a possible agent for Holland Life. I showed no interest at the time, as I compared selling Life Insurance with being a Fuller Brush salesman—somewhat below my aspirations. Besides, I was already employed, with several roles, in a seed company. During the winter months I was in the retail section for garden seeds. During the summer I oversaw consignment sales. After harvest in the fall, I traveled in the North Peace River area, visiting with farmers to evaluate field seeds for purity and making offers for the lots when acceptable. I enjoyed my work most of the time.

As a single person it had not been a problem for me to be on the road, away from Edmonton, for long periods of time. However, now that I was married and had additional responsibilities, my income was not quite enough. So, while not indicating much interest in our first meeting with the insurance agent, Mr. Terpstra, I did suggest he give me more information about what this position would entail. I also asked him to provide me with some reading material.

Upon receiving the requested reading material, I realized that it was not a question of whether I wanted to sell life insurance but of whether I had the necessary qualifications. When I contacted Klaas requesting further discussion, he was happy to oblige. He asked for more details about past employment, about my level of education and if I would agree to a psychological test to see if I was suitable for this position. I do not think I passed the test, but they seemed anxious to hire someone and I was offered a contract starting in January 1959. I accepted this challenge and started courses right away to prepare myself for this new venture.

My first year in the business went quite well; most of my sales were to family and friends. They knew and trusted me, and perhaps felt they should help me to get a good start. I even received a bonus at the end of the first year. It was enough to trade in my car, a second hand Ford with transmission problems, for a new 1960 Ford on a three-year payment contract. Our little house in Beverly (1000-sq.-ft. 2-bedroom with kitchen, living room and bath) had no garage. With this new car we had a better chance of a start when the temperature got to -30°F.

The following year I found the work more difficult. Contacting complete strangers and trying to build rapport with them was a great challenge.

In order to obtain a license to sell insurance, new agents were required to take special courses to comply with provincial law. To maintain it, they were required to take courses that helped to build up confidence and belief in the products sold.

When I first started making cold calls—that is, arriving without an appointment, not knowing the persons I was trying to contact for an interview—I was always afraid that I would be sent packing. Rather than making a phone call requesting an appointment, I would drive to a prospective client who might have been suggested to me by a friend, and ring the doorbell. One time, coming to someone's door, I chickened out. Scared of being rejected, I went to my car and went home. I have to build up my self-confidence, I told myself. There is nothing to fear; the worst that can happen is that they say, "No thanks". I also reminded myself that I had a very valuable product, one that would prevent the serious consequences of someone dying and leaving their spouse without income.

My confidence improved. And, as previous clients gave word-of-mouth referrals, prospective clients were easier to approach for an interview.

At this point, I started to use the telephone for my first contact more often. My name and that of the company were becoming better known, and interviews were more easily booked. After three years in Edmonton, the Holland Life Insurance management thought to promote me to a supervisory position, a task that involved recruiting new agents in Calgary and perhaps to eventually become a branch manager there.

In this, I failed. First off, I had not received the training needed for this position. Secondly, I found going out with prospective agents boring. I had no patience with the recruiting process, and I missed the independence I felt on the field. After a few years, I was ready to call it quits, but they offered to transfer me back to Edmonton.

It took several years to get back up to speed in terms of a clientele base. Other agents in Edmonton had taken over my portfolio during my absence, and I had to start from scratch again. Fortunately, I was known in the Dutch community, and my acquaintances felt more comfortable dealing with me than with non-Dutch agents.

Although I did better presenting our products in English, it helped to be able to interpret in Dutch when needed. It also helped to understand the Dutch culture and way of thinking. Often, the income of a Dutch immigrant client was not up to par with the average Canadian, and they were very frugal with their initial investments.

A few times I was instrumental in helping a new immigrant find employment, which made me a hero; those people never forgot. On one occasion, while having lunch in a restaurant, I met an old client from twenty years before. He greeted me with enthusiasm, saying that he remembered me as the one that took time out to introduce him to potential employers when he first came to Canada.

Once, my manager received a request from a Dutch immigrant that had settled in Fort St. John a year or two earlier. He had bought insurance in Holland from the same company and wanted upgrading. He was an engineer for an oil company, well-educated and fairly fluent in the English language. I was assigned to make contact with him and see what we could do.

Fort St. John, B.C., was 420 miles from Edmonton. I reasoned I should make a special trip to St. John, impressing upon him that he was a valuable customer of Holland Life. I made contact with him by telephone and informed him that I held his portfolio and would like to drive up to Fort St. John and see him the following week. That impressed him and we set a date. It was a risk. I was making a long drive with no idea whether I would successfully do business with him or not. Knowing only his age and profession, I prepared a few scenarios I could use for a quick presentation. Normally it would take two meetings: one for finding out what his needs or wants were, and another to come back with a well-thought-out solution.

A fellow agent in our office decided to come along for the ride to enjoy the scenery along the way and to watch me in action. Arriving at our prospective client's home at the appointed time, we were welcomed in by Mr. Van Dam and his wife. From experience, I knew I had to be a good listener. I usually started with small talk and gradually moved to the point of business at hand. I could tell this man needed to be listened to and admired, to boost his ego. The usual small talk normally lasted 5 to 10 minutes, but this time it took at least 30 minutes. Finally, we came to the point of our visit and got the conversation turned around to the business at hand.

Since our time was limited, I had made a quick diagnosis and now made a proposal on how to proceed. He asked some questions to show his intellectual acumen, and I, having predicted these questions, answered calmly with a carefully prepared response. However, to impress him and reassure him that I took his questions seriously, I closed my eyes pretending to be in deep thought. My companion, watching this interview, told me later that he thought I would get nowhere by closing my eyes.

By this time, my prospective client was satisfied that he was dealing with a bona fide insurance agent, someone of equal status, who understood his needs. During the interview, he had mentioned that he had a friend in Fort St John who also was an insurance agent but with a different company. I had ignored that and just stayed the course in my presentation, explaining that he was better off, in this case, to stay with one insurance company.

He accepted my proposal and I filled in two applications, one for him and one for his wife. We left there by eleven p.m. and drove 50 miles to Dawson Creek to stay the night. We celebrated our success with a drink, discussing the art of making sales. The commission was enough to pay for a month's income.

20

GOOD SAMARITAN?

It was the day before Christmas, sometime in the 60's. It was cold: about -20°C. As a life insurance agent, 1 had had a great year and was in a good mood. My colleagues and I decided to celebrate our success with a nice lunch at a fashionable club. During the fine meal, wine flowed freely, along with plenty of jokes, as we toasted ourselves, bragging about our ingenuity in making sales and just feeling really good.

Later, driving home all buoyant, I thought of the Christmas tree there, and my children's flushed, expectant faces. I looked forward to a happy evening, a lovely ending to an already perfect day.

As it was early afternoon when I arrived home, I checked the mail. There was cheque for $75, a small production bonus for the month. Thinking how nice it would be to replenish my recently spent cash, I got back into my car and drove to the bank.

Parking in front of the liquor store beside the bank, I noticed a few men sitting on a bench, hoisting paper bags intermittently to their faces. What a way to spend Christmas Eve, I mused, shaking my head. I paid no further attention to them. I entered the bank to cash my cheque, leaving my car unlocked. I was gone less than15 minutes.

Returning to the car and opening the door, I found an intoxicated man asleep with his head resting on the steering wheel. I shook him to awaken him, but he didn't budge. I tried shaking some more, to no avail. Thinking this was getting me nowhere, I grabbed him by the scruff of the neck and heaved him onto the icy pavement. To my shame I left him there, thinking he would get up shortly, or his drinking buddy would get up off the bench to look after him. Wheeling my way towards the parking lot exit, I peaked into the rearview mirror. A woman was walking over to him.

Suddenly, I felt very guilty and ashamed that I had not taken him to his home. By the time I left the parking lot, I was too embarrassed to turn back. I said to myself, You self-satisfied prude! Driving your warm, comfortable car with money in your pocket.

Are you not your brother's keeper? an inner voice said. Don't you remember times as a youth when you drove on treacherous roads after tipping a bottle? You were spared serious injury or death. So much for being taught to love your neighbour as yourself!

Driving home that day, and for months afterwards, the image of the man on the pavement kept returning to my mind, but it could not be undone.

A year or so later, on another bitterly cold evening, I had to make a call in the residential East Edmonton area. As usual, I left the car doors unlocked. Nobody would bother my car, parked blocks from the main road, I thought. There was nothing inside to interest a thief anyway.

What a surprise when I returned to my car about an hour later to discover two bare feet sticking out of the front door! By the amber light in the ceiling I saw a young woman lying in the front, her long, pitch-black hair spread over the seat. Was she alive? Badly hurt? Where did she come from? It was a quiet neighbourhood.

Wondering what to do, I called to her to see if she would respond. I heard groaning. I asked her if she could sit up. With some effort she gradually righted herself. She tried to put on her boots, but they were cold and stiff. I started the engine to warm the car.

I realized, Here is a second chance—an opportunity to show the compassion I should have shown in that earlier experience.

I asked her why she was unhappy. "How do you know I am unhappy?" she responded.

"1 guessed it, seeing the condition you are in and the look on your face," I replied.

I asked her where she was from, where she had been, and whether I could take her home. She told me she had been drinking at the Drake Hotel in Beverly, and her boyfriend had mistreated her. She had left him and been wandering the streets until she found my unlocked car.

I drove her downtown to where she lived.

I went home feeling I had repaid a debt. I could hold my head up. Still, I resolved to be more humble and thankful for good health and the ability to earn a decent living, and not to be condescending towards those not as blessed as I.

21

IMPATIENCE

All my life I have been a restless person. I have to be on the move, in action or planning action. I've been happiest when taking on something new—like a volunteer assignment—or planning a vacation or changing my vocation. I've loved being involved in sports and taking courses in such subjects as history, languages, and writing.

I never seem to take much time in researching how to proceed; I just dive in. Once into my newest undertaking, I channel all my energy into it. My total immersion can sometimes be at the expense of other aspects of my life, such as work or family.

One year I spent a great deal of time pursuing running as a sport. I competed in five- and ten-mile races and ran some marathons (26-miles runs). I was doing well amongst my peers, and received a lot of praise and encouragement. This motivated me to try to do even better. In total, that year, I ran more than two thousand miles. That was in 1972 (the year I turned 43).

During that same year my work performance suffered; both my productivity and my income decreased by about 40 %. But I was having fun! My weight then was only 163 lbs (74kg) on a 6 ft frame (your height). I was skinny as a runt!

Impatience hampers careful planning. Even as I write this story my mind races ahead of my pen and I forget to think about grammar or how to construct the next thought. This, of course, results in having to rewrite.

It also means I probably forget to include many interesting details which might make my story a better one.

Traffic tickets—and I admit and lament the fact that I have had many of them—are another result of my impatience. Speeding is a bad habit but one I find difficult to control when driving a modern vehicle on a beautiful stretch of quiet highway. (My competitive nature is to blame there, too.)

Impatience has caused me other embarrassments. In the past, while waiting in the car for my wife and children to join me in driving somewhere, I'd frequently grow so impatient that I would beep the car horn. Afterwards I'd apologize, but the damage was done. Years later I had an accident resulting in the loss of one of my legs and I was on crutches for three years. I couldn't drive and was dependent on my wife, Grace, for transportation. In the early months of crutch use, I was slow at getting from the house to the car. On a few occasions, in fun, Grace would beep the horn just to let me know how it felt to have the shoe on the other foot. I laughed about it. I had it coming.

Once, when I bought a new car, I was again reminded of my impatience. Whenever this car needed warranty repairs, I was given priority service; I did not have to make an appointment beforehand. After several instances of jumping the queue, however, it became obvious that this would not last. One day, I went to the dealership without an appointment, as usual. As I strode in, expectation and annoyance were clear in my body language. The shop foreman looked up from his desk and, seeing me, turned around and hollered to the mechanics, "Everybody stop what you are doing—Francis is here!" Well, again, I had a good laugh. I needed that message.

Nevertheless, I've feel that I have used my restless energy to my advantage. Whenever problems arose, whether they were small aggravations such as a repair job around the house or a communication breakdown between me and another person, I dealt with it as soon as possible. My attitude was: fix what is broken, or clear up misunderstandings and apologize immediately. This way my mind is clear to move on to other things on my agenda.

IMPATIENCE

Restlessness and impatience were also useful attributes in my career as a life insurance agent. My mother used to say, "Just watch the cat. It will sit hunched for hours to catch its prey." Well, when making a presentation to a prospective customer, my body language tended to signal a subtle, if not clear message of urgency and importance. Maybe that's not what my mother had in mind, but it evidently worked well because I was fairly successful in my sales career.

22

THE COWBOY

It was 1967 when my father in Holland sent us an invitation to my parents' 55th wedding anniversary. Grace and I were excited about traveling to Holland to meet our families and share in the festivities.

Grace had never traveled by air before and felt apprehensive about boarding a plane. Since I had flown a number of times as part of my job, visiting our head office in Toronto, I thought Grace would get over her fear of flying if I booked a trip with several flights. The first flight I booked was leaving Edmonton in the morning and stopping in Toronto. There we would change planes and take an old, vibrating four-engine DC3 to Montreal. Finally, we would take a bigger plane to Amsterdam via London, England. Planning that, I realized later, was not a smart thing to do. Mind you, in the sixties there were no direct flights to Europe from Edmonton; usually it would take at least one stopover.

By the time we got to Montreal, Grace had had enough of traveling by air, especially when she looked at the big aircraft we were about to board. She didn't think it could stay up, let alone get off the ground. I assured her that she did not need to worry since this aircraft had four big powerful jet engines, but I held her hand as the bulky plane lifted off into the sky. A little later, after she'd had a glass of wine with her dinner, she managed a nap.

I must confess I had an ulterior motive in taking this route. In my younger days I had worked as a ranch hand and was familiar with horses. I considered myself a real cowboy. I used to drive cattle from the outer ranch area to the ranch coral on a fast horse called Pete. In western Canada people know about the horses and cattle drives of earlier days, but not so in eastern Canada or Europe. Therefore, I had in mind to show off what a cowboy looks like in his authentic regalia. I thought I could at least put on a good act. Grace thought I was daft. She even threatened to take a different seat.

We left for Holland in early May, with me in my newly-acquired duds: cowboy boots, jeans, an open shirt with shining buttons, a denim jacket and a large Stetson. I was not conspicuous boarding our first flight in Edmonton. It wasn't until we arrived in Toronto that I got some second glances. In Montreal I got more extensive observation. I could tell folks appreciated coming in contact with a real cowboy.

When we arrived at Heathrow airport, safe and sound, we went to the waiting area for our next flight to Amsterdam. It was there that I was admired the most. Several people looked me over from head to toe and a few teenage girls walked by a couple times and giggled.

Needing still more exposure, I visited the bar, where the locals hang out, to have a drink. I sat down near a man wearing a top hat and reading a magazine. I greeted him with, "Howdy, Sir". He gave me the blink of an eye and paid no further attention to me. I tested him with an offer to buy him a whisky on the rocks. It did not work. *So much for camaraderie*, I thought.

It was time to board our next flight to Amsterdam, a short one. Disembarking, we came down the ladder onto the tarmac. Walking towards the customs area, I saw my parents standing on the second-floor balcony watching the people coming off the airplane. They did not recognize us.

After going through customs, we climbed the stairs to where they were standing, still watching to see if more aircraft would arrive with us on board. When I was directly behind them, I asked who they were looking for. My elderly mother turned, then gasped and said, "Is that you my boy?"

"Yes, Mum," I answered, and we embraced as if I were her prodigal son.

The following week there was the big anniversary celebration in the village pub. It started with dinner followed by speeches and the reading of a few poems about the past by family members and relatives. My contribution was singing some cowboy songs. I wore my cowboy attire again and sang "Home on the Range" and a few other Country & Western songs. The performance was well received. One uncle, who had visited Canada the year before, was all excited. His jaw dropped wide open, as if he wanted to drink in the songs.

After the family festivities ended inside, we went outside and sat on the patio, where we were entertained with a short concert by the village music corps in honour of our parents' wedding anniversary. I felt so intoxicated by their music that I emptied my glass of wine in short order and, in casual cowboy style, threw the empty glass into a flowerbed beside me. Later, a rumour went around about "that goofy Canadian" who had lost his manners.

23

HIKING IN THE WILDS, PART I

I love the outdoors. In particular, I like hiking in the Rocky Mountains, in Jasper National Park, near my home in Edmonton, Alberta.

I was introduced to this sport through a hiking and backpacking course, which taught survival skills and environmental awareness, among other outdoor skills. It improved my skill in dealing with obstacles that might arise while in the wilderness, and was a real boost to my self-confidence.

Backcountry hiking requires a lot of preparation. The most important thing is to be physically fit. Depending on the distance of your intended hike, a backpack can weigh between 35 and 50 lbs; it takes a lot of stamina to carry it. Planning your route, one must consult a map to be aware of the topography and possible obstacles, such as fordable creeks which, after crossing and after a heavy rain, become un-fordable rivers, preventing you from coming back the same way. In higher elevations you might encounter snow that could obscure your trail and take you off course. Also, you must know what to do when meeting a black or grizzly bear on your path.

Specific equipment is also needed, such as a well-fitting backpack. Besides suiting your body size and build, it must have sufficient capacity for all the paraphernalia needed on your trip. It is a good idea to have a few extra days' supply of food, in case of delays in reaching your destination. It is advisable to carry a first aid kit, too, as there are no medical clinics on the forested mountain heights.

Always let the park wardens know where you are going and when are you are expecting to be back. Also let friends know of your plans.

Finally, it is advisable to start with a short hike the first time out, say a couple of days long. Your body needs to adjust to the weight on your shoulders. If the weight is great, even padded straps will bite into your shoulders. Also, you need to break in your hiking boots. Make sure they are well-fitted, as you don't want blisters on your feet the first day out on the trail. When your body and mind are broken in by this experience, you might feel comfortable and confident enough to do longer trips.

My debut hike was in midsummer, 1970, with a fellow worker named Fred. He was a sturdy fellow who had a lot of self-confidence. As it turned out, he was not as skilful as he made himself out to be; while he looked more robust than I, he tired much sooner.

We decided on an overnight backpacking trip. We left our car at a campground called Rock Lake. Shortly after taking off we had to cross the fast-running Rock creek. Our pant legs got wet, even though we rolled them up above our knees. We arrived at our designated campground near a ranger station, about eight miles from where we left our car, shortly after lunch.

It was still early enough in the day for me to leave my backpack at the campground and hike further. I wanted to seek out a waterfall that was supposedly a few miles further up the trail and I thought it should be fairly easy to hike the extra distance without a cumbersome backpack. My companion did not share my idea and chose to go fishing in a nearby creek, instead.

Off I went, full of confidence. Unfortunately, I did not realize how much energy I had already expended in the first four hours, during the heat of the day. Now, although I was without a heavy backpack, I noticed that the hilly terrain and higher elevation were tiring me out much faster than expected. I had lost a lot of body fluid earlier, under the heavy load. I kept drinking water from small, running creeks I passed. After about three miles, I felt myself getting weaker and decided to turn back and join Fred, hoping he would have supper started.

No such luck. I was now exhausted and still felt dehydrated. My companion was nowhere in sight. Feeling disconsolate, I sat down, consciously drinking more to replace the lost fluids. After waiting for some time I started cooking by myself, using rice, spices and some sausage for a simple meal. My friend finally showed up, very happily carrying several small trout. He had thought he would surprise me with freshly-caught fish for supper. I had difficulty showing enthusiasm for his catch of trout. Since I had supper waiting, we ate the prepared meal and saved the fish for breakfast.

We went to bed early and arose when the birds and squirrels woke us up with their morning chirps and chatter. Despite a good rest, I did not feel sufficiently energized to resume hiking back to our car with my backpack. We drank some water then fried some bacon and added the filleted trout to the frying pan. The aroma alone made my stomach growl. Soon I was drooling. The meal was most delicious. We ate every bite, using the last of the bread to sop up the fat. As my energy level came back up from the depletion of the previous day, I felt reinvigorated.

Looking at the sky, we realized we needed to make haste. Evidently, a storm was brewing, and we had to get across the creek before the rain made it swell to a river that we could not cross.

We barely made it in time. We crossed the creek and were relieved to get to our car just before the rain came down. We made it safely back to our respective homes without any trouble, except for the painful, blistered feet of my friend.

24

HIKING IN THE WILDS,
PART II

I was initiated into backpacking in 1972 when I went on a short hike with a colleague. From then on, I was hooked.

The following year I asked my daughters, Carolyn and Linda, to join me on a three-day hike into Jasper Park's mountainous backcountry. My wife, mother of our daughters, was not interested in carrying a backpack. She was even less interested in meeting up with bears and mosquitoes. Mosquitoes seem to favour her blood. Even if there is only one, it will find her and suck her blood until it is bloated and has difficulty staying airborne.

We drove to Pyramid Lake campground, about fifteen miles northeast of Jasper. We left our car at a campground, hoisted our backpacks onto our shoulders and started off for Snake Indian Falls, some 8 miles further north. We did not meet any scary animals to frighten us, only a few squirrels and singing birds. We did, however, watch for droppings that would tell us what type of animals frequented that trail.

Our packs were not heavy on this relatively short hike. My daughters were in good spirits and enjoyed the excitement on the trail, with all the natural beauty of its landscape.

We reached our destination, a campground near Snake Indian Falls, in late afternoon. (Those were the falls I missed the year before, when I had gone hiking with Fred. I didn't know it at the time, but I had gone in the wrong direction from the camp.) We put up our tent and cooked our supper on a small fire. Next morning we visited the majestic falls. The water drops about a hundred feet before continuing as a fast-flowing river.

On our return the following morning, a couple miles into the hike, we came around a bend on the trail and saw a grizzly bear not far ahead of us on the trail. We knew it was a grizzly by the hump on its neck. It scared us, mostly because this type of bear is much more dangerous than the black bear. We backtracked, hoping the bear could not see us. Carolyn was very frightened; she went scurrying up a skinny tree and stayed there, even though it was too small to do any good. I told everyone to take off their backpacks and put them in front of us, reasoning that if the bear did come closer he might be content with the packs and we could make a run for it. I asked a young fellow by the name of Jim Stokes, who was from Ohio and had joined us on the trail, to whistle to alert the bear of our presence. At the surprising sound, the bear reared up on his hind legs, sniffed the air and took off. We waited some minutes before carrying on and seeing where the bear had left his footprints in the soft, sandy trail.

We moved on to the campground of Pyramid Lake, some ten-mile distance from Highway 16. Highway 16 is a narrow road, accessible northbound or southbound on alternate hours for one-way traffic only.

Pyramid Lake was an attractive campground favoured by a younger crowd who found it a convenient place to quench their thirst with beer or other liquids without close supervision by park rangers. Sure enough, as soon as we got there, I spotted a park bench loaded with beer bottles. Being thirsty, too, and very tired, I hankered for a brew, but resisted the urge to ask them to share their refreshments with me. Besides, I disapprove of fellows that go into the park solely to have a party without enjoying the beauty of God's creation.

I became even more annoyed when they stayed up by the campfire until midnight, imbibing more, cutting wood and making a lot of noise in general. We were tired and wanted a good rest so that we could get up and head home early the next morning.

I felt tempted, before leaving in the morning, to blow our car horn long enough to awaken those who had kept us awake and make them come out of their tents. However, my daughters discouraged me from making a ruckus.

Instead, as we left, we meditated on the thrill of hiking and decided to re-ignite our newly-acquired passion the following year. All the excitement, plus the grandeur of the scenery at the waterfall, made this trip a rather intoxicating experience in the healthy sense.

Back home, we needed to get cleaned up. Although Grace was very happy to see us back safely, her nostrils were not; she suggested we take some fresh clothes and go the Glenora Club for a steam bath and a shower. We were happy to comply. In the meantime she prepared a most delicious meal to celebrate our safe return.

25

BACKPACKING
(1972-1986)

I was initiated into backpacking in 1972 when I went on a short hike with a friend. From that point on, I was hooked.

The following year I asked my daughters Carolyn and Linda (ages 15 and 16 at the time) to join me on a three-day hike into Jasper Park's mountainous back country. We started at Pyramid Lake, traveling north towards Snake Indian Falls where we camped for two days.

That experience was so exciting for the girls that we planned a 10-day wilderness trek of 103 miles on a trail known as the "North Boundary Trail". Early in the spring of 1974, we prepared ourselves for this extensive and arduous trek. For a couple of months, I had the girls (then aged 16 and 17) get up each morning at 6:00 for a workout of a 3-mile run. This would ensure that they developed strong legs and stamina. A few weeks before our departure we put books into their backpacks and walked around, first in the basement and later in the back alley, to strengthen their backs. It hardened their shoulder muscles, enabling them to carry the weight and stand the pressure of the shoulder straps.

On the appointed day in the last week of June, we had our cousin Nico drive us to Rock Lake, northwest of Hinton. From there we picked up the North Boundary Trail, destined for the base of Mount Robson.

We started off with great excitement, studying the trail for telltale signs of wildlife such as bear droppings and the like. After a few hours we reached Rock Creek, which was swollen to a threatening volume due to recent rainfall. It was about 30 feet wide and looked scary, so I used a pole as a crutch and a balance against the fast-flowing current and ventured in to check its depth. We attached a rope to a tree as a safety line and stepped into the stream. I led the way, Carolyn followed and Linda brought up the rear, all of us holding onto the rope. The water nearly reached the top of the girls' legs. We reached the other side without a problem, and, as it was a warm and sunny, our wet pants dried on our bodies as we traveled on. We saw a few elk but no bears, and we reached our first night's target camp of Willow Creek safely.

To minimize carrying weight we had taken only one two-person tent plus a plastic sheet for me to sleep under. The first night under the stars, the mosquitoes were relentless in stinging me and sucking my blood. By 4:00 a.m. I gave up trying to sleep and crawled in with the girls. They were both sleeping in one direction and I went in between them the other way with my shoulders between their pairs of legs. Like sardines in a can, we slept comfortably and repeated the arrangement each night for the duration of our trip. I would never have lasted with only the plastic covering given all the rain we experienced later.

Day 2: For breakfast we had some instant coffee, and a slice of rye bread with cheese. Breaking camp, we hoisted our packs on our still-aching shoulders. Our next campground was only 8 miles away, but far enough for bodies still adjusting to the packs. Mine weighed about 45 lbs. and each of the girls' about 35 lbs. Our bodies were also adjusting to changes in elevation. We were traveling fairly high above sea level, 4000 ft and higher. This meant the air was thinner, requiring more air to get enough oxygen; we were huffing and puffing. Nevertheless, we reached our camp in mid-afternoon.

Under a light drizzle of rain, we settled down. The girls were happy to shed their packs and massaged each other's shoulders to relieve the stiffness. Supper consisted of soup and rye bread with cheese and pepperoni sausage. We slept like babies.

Day 3: A sunny day. We crossed several creeks, balancing ourselves on logs that were lying across the creeks. We were climbing higher, and our pack straps seemed to be digging ever deeper into our shoulders. We rested for an hour for a lunch of macaroni and cheese. Everything tasted good on our hike, as we were burning a lot of calories and had fantastic appetites.

We covered about 17 miles that day and were bone tired. Linda had to stop and rest about half a mile from our evening camp. Carolyn and I went ahead to drop our packs at a campsite and then went back for Linda. I shouldered Linda's pack and the three of us made it to our camp. The mosquitoes welcomed us in great numbers and shared the hot food we prepared over our campfire. We ate the food, including some mosquitoes, with great relish. Having our camp ready for the night, we enjoyed the peace and scenery. We studied our map for the next day's trek, and noted a steep climb from where we were camping. We ended the day with a few songs and hot chocolate.

Day 4: We'd thought this day would be a little easier since it was only 8 miles to our next camp, but two miles into our hike our trail disappeared under spring run-off which had turned the terrain into a wet marshland. I decided to circumvent the marsh by following the hillside. A few hundred yards along this hill I had the girls rest while I scouted for the trail. While scouting around I blazed my trail, using a small axe to strip a little bark off some of the trees along the way, so as not to get lost. To my dismay, however, the search was cut short when I spied a young black bear under a tree some distance below us. I did not mention it to the girls for fear it might make them uneasy, but I suggested we backtrack and wade through the water where the trail was supposed to be. This meant we'd also have to cross a fast-flowing stream, too wide to jump over. I managed to cut down a tree, big enough to lie across the stream, for us to scuttle over. My haste was obvious; the girls wondered why I refused to allow them to stop nibble bakers' chocolate as we usually did for a treat a few hours into the day. Finally I told them about the bear, and they understood and felt relieved that the potential threat was well behind us.

Day 5: Thursday. Snake Indian Pass. Carolyn wrote in her journal, "We climbed and climbed through mud and snow, crossing a fast-flowing creek. Our boots and pants were sopping wet when we arrived at the locked warden's cabin."

Snake Indian Pass is at an altitude of 7500 feet. We could barely make out the trail, so we followed what appeared to be a telegraph line running approximately adjacent to our trail. The snow, in places near the top, was knee deep.

Coming over the top of the ridge was a great relief; from here on, it would be all downhill. At our camp, near the warden's cabin, we made a nice big celebratory fire. The sun was out, and Linda and Carolyn put on their shorts, washed their jeans and laid them out to dry by the fire. We all felt delighted to have reached this milestone of our expedition, the halfway mark.

Then, suddenly, we saw very dark clouds approaching and it started to snow like crazy, big flakes. It was at about this point that I realized we were probably about a month too early for this trek. I quickly put a plastic sheet over the tent, tying it down with some spare rope. Linda and Carolyn, in their shorts, went into the tent and into their sleeping bags to keep warm. I went to cut more firewood and kept a big fire blazing. Luckily, the snowfall lasted less than an hour and we were able to cook and enjoy a good supper outside.

Day 6: In the morning there was still some snow on the ground, but we broke camp and headed towards our next destination. The weather was crisp as we traveled slowly downhill. Because of the snow, we lost our trail again at one point. We had been traveling upwards following a steep rocky avalanche path, which seemed like a dry riverbed. After about half an hour we realized we were going in the wrong direction and turned back. Fortunately, we soon found the right trail again.

Day 7: Uneventful, just making nice progress. We had seen the occasional porcupine around our evening campsite. Because of them we took care to put our hiking boots inside our tent; the porcupine could be attracted to the salty leather and chew on our boots.

Day 8: That evening we camped on the flat pebbly riverbed beside Smoky River in a gorge between two mountains. I took a bath in the river, a very fast one, with my backside in the ice-cold water, while the girls kept a fire going. They averted their eyes and just handed me a towel so I could dry myself and warm up by the fire before putting on dry clothes.

That night it rained. It seemed like it was coming down by the bucketful. I was worried about the river overflowing its banks and flooding our campsite. The girls slept peacefully, but I stuck my hand out through the tent flaps several times during the night testing for water on our campground. Next morning we broke camp in the rain and walked a wet trail to our next campground, 14 miles from the end of our expedition.

The campground was named Adolphus, and there was only one other camper there, a man named Roger. He was a teacher at the University of Alberta, and was impressed by our long hike. When he learned that we had no transportation home the next day, he offered us a ride to Edmonton.

Day 9: We broke camp early for the long journey down the Mount Robson trail. We passed Berg Lake where a number of campers had spent the night. A bit further down we witnessed a chunk of ice from a glacier caving into the lake, making a sound like thunder

The weather was nice but the trail slippery in places from the previous day's rain. In some areas where the trail was particularly muddy we saw hikers with heavy packs grunting and groaning up the steep slope. Our packs were 10 lbs. lighter since our start and we felt buoyant coming down the hill. The last 5 miles or so was on level ground on a path covered with wood chips. Linda wrote in her journal, "I will never forget the last 5 miles. It occurred to me that it was as if we were in a fairy tale picture. Pine needles covered the ground, a rainbow radiated through the trees. The beauty of what looked to us like a rain forest was breathtaking. The trail was so neat and dry, bridges over the smallest trickle of streams, you'd expect the trail was developed for women travelers in high heels!" We found it hilarious when we heard a bell's jingling, supposedly to ward off bears. To our ears the harsh-sounding bells sounded as if we would meet a lost cow!"

Later that day we dined in Jasper, to treat Roger for our ride home. We ate at a dining table with a white tablecloth, even though we were still in our stinky clothes. It must have been difficult for the waiter to endure.

We were very happy and thankful to get home and proud of our achievements. The sisters said they'd do it again if given the opportunity. We did have other opportunities on different trails around Jasper Park, but only one daughter could come on those trips to join her Dad.

My own last hike was into Tonquin Valley in 1986.

26

GOING TO COLLEGE

It was with great excitement and expectation that The King's College (as it was known then) opened its doors in September, 1979, in Edmonton. We were thankful that the long laid plans for the college had finally come to fruition. It had been more than ten years of making donations and wondering if our Christian community could and would support such a great undertaking. It had been a leap of faith for all concerned just as it had been when we started the Christian elementary school and, later, the high school. The Christian community always struggled before being ready to accept the cost of Christian education. We hated to part with our hard-earned money, especially when our incomes were very modest. However, the call to have our children be instructed in a Christian worldview overruled our worry of affordability. God blessed us with incomes more than sufficient to do the job.

Now the college was open. With some trepidation, I, too, applied, as an adult student, to enter this new institution. I did not know if I could handle listening to lectures and writing term papers, but I wanted to try. In my youth I had abandoned higher education, thinking I didn't have the intellect. I was also a restless person and did not think it was important. (This was during the Second World War.) But now, doing quite well in my business career, I had a desire to do more than earn a good living. I wanted to have a better understanding of my role in life—in creation— and in the workplace

I used to be somewhat in awe of those who had a PhD. degree. That lessened over time, mind you, especially one time when a psychiatrist was in my office telling me how I should do my work. I should have obliged him; he was a client. Instead I was a bit foolish, recklessly asking him if he would lie down on my couch and accept my diagnosis! Not surprisingly, he left. His advice illustrated to me that we might be experts in certain fields, but sometimes we lack knowledge in ordinary things in life.

Still, I was a bit intimidated by the thought of higher education. Also, in undertaking this new venture as a part-time student at King's, I was somewhat self-conscious about how these younger students would view this 50-year-old gent. I needn't have worried; they thought it was 'cool' and gave me credit for being an older person who could see the benefits of broadening one's horizons through knowledge.

History was my favourite subject; I had already read books on Canadian history, learning about Canada's roots and its struggle to become a nation. Dr. Harry Groenewold was the history professor at King's. Our first course was Western Civilization. It covered the time before and after Christ, including the Roman period, the mediaeval times, the renaissance and the reformation era. I enjoyed the last the most. I learned as much about myself as I did about kings, potentates and the church. When reading about personalities in history I could identify with them and realized that, like the rulers of those times, all of us are sinners in need of God's grace.

I passed the first few exams with a B average. Good enough. I felt encouraged to take some more courses in other fields. These I completed with varying degrees of success. I had a difficult time in English and Music.

English, being my second language, caused more than a few headaches. My completed essay papers were usually returned with a lot of red ink, not because their content but for sentence form and punctuation! I used to handwrite my essays first, and then ask my secretary to type them, admonishing her to watch out for mistakes in grammar. Invariably she would fear making changes. I would read her typed version, make a few changes myself and have her type the paper again. Still, there would be red ink. I changed to a typist who majored in English, but there would still be red ink!

In Music I could not read notes, nor could I remember which composer had written each piece. Dr. Kloppers was kind, and I did enjoy the classical music, so he let me pass.

Taking two courses per semester for a few years was a slow way to earn a degree. The thought came to me that I might take a sabbatical from work. I used to be envious of pastors and professors who took sabbaticals. Now I thought, Why not a businessman also? I knew that Dordt College, in Iowa, USA, was offering winter semester courses in Amsterdam, Holland, in history, art, literature and business. I applied and, with the blessing of King's College, was welcomed to join them.

My wife, Grace, and I rented an apartment within walking distance of the university in Amsterdam, the Netherlands. We enjoyed visiting our ancestral homes and our siblings, and became reacquainted with Dutch history.

Returning to King's the next semester, I challenged myself by taking courses at a more advanced level. Indeed, they were a challenge. I found philosophy, in particular—though interesting—to be confusing and difficult. Once, I wrote a poem for Dr. Schuurman to appeal to his sense of humour and to divert his attention from my miserable essay. He accepted it with good grace.

Biology was another required course, and this one I was permitted to take at Athabasca University. I took a course in botany called "Wild Flowers in Alberta." I thought this course, held outdoors in the Kananaskis Mountains, would be invigorating and not too difficult. It turned out to be one of the most challenging of all. There were ten of us students, putting in ten-hour days of intense study, spending half the time in the field and half in the laboratory. The Latin names of species, families and related species made my head spin. A fellow student, Rita, also from King's College, was helpful with tips and encouragement. After I finished the course, and my brain had time to rest, I could say it was a great and rewarding experience.

Finally the last semester in winter 1987 came to an end, and, together with three other students, I graduated from The King's College with a bachelor's degree in history. The college also celebrated a milestone at this time. The government of Alberta had finally given King's the degree-granting accreditation it had sought. From then on, it was, officially, King's University College.

The graduation ceremonies were held in a United Church at 144th Street and 107th Avenue. It was a very momentous event for me, personally, and certainly for the rest of the students, staff and supporting community as well.

27

COPPERMINE RIVER ADVENTURE

In 1982, I was invited by a man named Gordon to participate on a 640 km (400 mile) canoe trip from Lac La Grass to the town of Coppermine on the Arctic coast. Although I was not familiar with this river, I had a great interest in the Northwest Territories and wanted to learn more about the Dene Indian Nation and the Eskimo settlements on the Artic coast. Therefore, I accepted the invitation.

I had learned some of the history of the Dene Indian Nation by reading the journals of Samuel Hearne's expedition in 1772. These journals describe the adventures of Hearne and his Dene guides as they trekked from the Hudson Bay area to Coppermine, a distance in excess of 2000 miles.

I had met Gordon, a fellow backpacker, while hiking in the Mount Robson area. Gordon had noticed my adeptness at carrying a backpack in the mountains and thought I would be a good prospect to come along on this adventurous undertaking. He downplayed the skill needed for the trip saying I would learn quickly enough. I was not so sure.

Returning home from that previous backpacking trip, I had come in contact with Henry, an acquaintance who had previous river-paddling experience. Henry and I trained every Saturday that summer to be ready for July 22nd when our group of six would leave in three 17-foot long canoes, two paddlers in each.

A trip like this takes a lot of planning. One needs to be in good physical shape, ready to face some hardships. One had to be able to manoeuvre raging rapids, and have the survival skills to recover from accidental rollover in frigid water. The weather is also a challenge, especially when rain and wind tie you to shore for a day or two. On warm days, black flies and mosquitoes attack relentlessly.

You also need a month's worth of supplies to tide you over in the event of bad weather or other mishaps. Food supplies must be in watertight bags. Fortunately, fresh, clear water is available on the trip by scooping it up from the river, over the edge of the canoe.

Another important aspect of this type of travel is compatibility with fellow canoeists—something I became aware of once we were on our way. Our group included Gordon, Robert and Les who were schoolteachers; Henry, an artist; my companion, Basha, a registered nurse who brought a large metal box of first aid supplies; and me, an insurance agent adept at paddling. Basha, the lone female in our party, withstood many interested glances. Two of the others and I were morning persons always ready for departure first thing in the morning. The other three stayed longer at the campfire in the evenings and had difficulty arising the next day. This created some friction.

Our trip began with a nice meal the night before our departure at the Wild Cat Café in Yellowknife. The next day we chartered a twin otter float plane to take us to our point of departure at Lac La Grass, 100 miles north of Yellowknife. On Day One we pulled our canoes over patches of ice on the river. The water temperature was no more than 5 degrees Celsius. The next day we faced our first set of rapids. They were scary but we managed them without incident.

The mosquitoes in the North are legendary. They come in droves like a bunch of Kamikaze. It was a good thing we had mosquito head nets (a must to prevent you from going berserk)!

Prior to entering the rough rapids, one has to expose one's derriere in order to change into a wetsuit. One's bottom then becomes a target for those true blue bloodsuckers!

One evening my tent partner forgot to shake the mosquitoes from his jacket before entering the tent. When I woke up the following morning, those pesky insects had taken so much blood from me that they had difficulty staying airborne. They reminded me of B52 bombers and air strikes.

There is solitude in that great expanse of the Northwest Territories. And the majesty of it all! It makes men aware of their own insignificance. The distances are immense, flowers grow in soil only a foot deep above the permafrost, and lichens growing on wind-swept rocks provide nourishment for the reindeer. (In 1821-22, Sir John Franklin ate some of these lichens to prevent starvation.) The water is clear and pure, delicious to drink, and never more than a few steps from your campsite.

Fishing is a real treat. After leaving Yellowknife, there was no meat except for some smoked sausage and chunks of cheese. We caught trout and later grayling (plenty of them to suit our needs), a wonderful respite from dehydrated food. At our halfway point, we were guests of Max Ward's fishing lodge on the river. He treated us to an overnight stay complete with showers and meals. In repayment, three of us helped him roof a house he was building at his tent camp.

By chance, a colleague of mine was also visiting at the camp and invited me to go fishing with him for a while. I rarely go fishing and accepted his invitation. Within a short time I caught an eighteen-pound trout. My friend, Bill, sat in the stern and watched me pull it out; with the sun's reflection of the fish on the water, it seemed twice its size.

Bill was so excited I was afraid his heart medication might fail him. His comment, after the catch, was, "Don't tell me you are not a fisherman!" But I knew I was just lucky. I offered to let him take it home, so he could brag about "HIS" fish.

We encountered a few minor mishaps along the way. One canoe tipped twice in icy water. Wetsuits saved the occupants from serious cool-down or shock. After a spill, we would go to shore and build a fire for a warm-up before we started on our way again.

One day we ran into a storm that was strong enough to cause 3-foot waves. We went on shore and set up camp. The wind made putting up our tents very difficult. I was already tired from battling the waves and was the first one to climb into Basha's larger tent to eat some peanuts and take a nap. Others had cut some wood and started a fire. Then more men dove into the tent, and it was my turn to be on watch. I cooked a meal and served it to the others inside—a gesture for which I was applauded.

I also want to share an incident about our leader (I had another expression for the word leader, but will not mention the epithet). He was one of the three who were tardy some mornings. He was also in the habit of having one last cup of tea before departure.

The event occurred on a day when it was my turn to prepare breakfast—consisting of Bannock—and then ensure everything was ready for take-off after the meal. On this particular morning, after breakfast, our leader slipped away into the bushes to relieve his bowels. In the meantime, we delayed dampening the campfire in order to keep his teacup warm. I told my fellow sojourners to forget the tea; we were breaking up—no time for an extra tea break. This did not sit well with our leader—the overture had not been quite genteel—but the message was received and there were no further reverberations.

The day before our arrival at Coronation Gulf and the town of Coppermine, we came to the "Bloody Falls". They were so named after the massacre of two dozen Eskimos by their Indian rivals, the tribe who had guided Samuel Hearne to this coast in 1772. These falls were very rough; we had to portage, carrying all our belongings, including the canoes, and making two trips of about one kilometre each way. We had had a late start that morning, and I was hopping mad about the delay. There was no love lost between some of us. We reached the Coppermine beach at 11 pm, fortunately still in daylight. An Eskimo who had just come from a seal hunt approached us and gave us some fresh liver from his catch. We made a campfire on the spot, spiced and fried the liver, and ate to our stomach's content. How delicious that was! I could smile again.

Our arrival in the town of Coppermine coincided with the Northern Games. Eskimos from far and wide showed their skills at seal skinning, fish cleaning, high kicking and more. There was a dance that night. The hall was full of natives with unfamiliar profiles and different scents that discouraged me from taking part. Besides, I think my dance style would have been out of synch.

It took 2 hours to fly from Coppermine to Yellowknife, where we stayed overnight. The next day we flew back to Edmonton. The total flight time from Coppermine to Edmonton was about 4 hours. By contrast, on land it took two days in a pickup truck (driven by Robert, my tent partner and owner of one of the canoes) plus four weeks of paddling. Both ways, by land and by air, it was a journey of 640 km. Our thanks to God for a safe passage; we had crossed a few places where previous voyageurs had lost their lives.

28

THE EURO-RAIL PASS

In June of 1979, Grace and I attended the Canada Life Convention in London, England. From there we took an overnight ferry from Harrich to the port of "Hook of Holland" from there by train to Delft, We staid in the Netherlands, for a ten-day visit with our parents and siblings. Grace opted to return home from there as we had left our teenaged daughter, Marianne, alone at home. As for me, I was filled with an urge to see more of Europe's culture and history.

Before leaving home, Grace and I had discussed the idea of traveling with a Euro-Rail Pass to neighbouring countries, but in the end she declined this type of adventure. However, I had received a $1500 inheritance from my mother and felt this would adequately finance my trip needs. I shared my plan with my father, 91, who lived in a senior citizens' home. I was somewhat apprehensive about mentioning it, since he had always lived a fairly frugal life despite his success in business. I must add that he survived stressful times, having fathered 12 children and weathered the depression.

So, instead of telling him I was planning to "bum around Europe on Mother's legacy", I carefully explained my desire to study Europe's history and visit different places in "memory of mother." Aware of my restlessness and need to spread my wings, my father had, from time to time in the past, given me his blessing for such ventures. He did so once again.

The Euro-rail Pass was good for three weeks, first class, and I intended to visit France, Spain, Italy and Greece. So, having said good-bye to Grace in Delft.

I shouldered my backpack and took a train to my first stop, Paris. I had studied French for about six months before my trip and looked forward to putting it to use.

After we crossed the border into Belgium, a French lady boarded the train in Brussels and entered my compartment. After the usual "Bonjour, Madame" and "Bonjour, Monsieur", I spoke my first French sentence, which had taken me several minutes to formulate in my mind. It must have sounded fluent because she loosed a flood of words, and gave me her repertoire of knowledge about what she thought I was interested in. When there was a hiatus in her verbal torrent and I had formulated the next question that I thought related to a few words I had fished out, she was off again with what seemed like an endless stream of words interspersed with "Mon Dieu".

This was my First Baptism or total immersion, you might say, of the French language. It occurred to me that if I had suggested rooming and boarding with her, she would have accepted, just so she could use me as a receiver of the river of words that rushed past me like the fast moving train we were traveling in. Perhaps after a few months or more of exposure I would have been able to identify some of the words from her lighting-fast speech. At this point, though, my vocabulary was not even sufficiently developed to ask her to slow down. She took leave of the train at Le Gare du Nord in Paris with just a "Bon Nuit".

Shouldering my backpack again I took the underground train to the "Quartier Latin" (the Latin quarter of Paris) where many university students lived and where inexpensive lodging and some interesting eateries could be found.

The next day I found one of those bistros which looked quite lively, where you could see and smell some attractive dishes. The decor was very simple, with long tables and benches. After finding an available seat, I looked over the menu and then at what other people were eating, trying to match what they had with what I read on the menu. It made little sense to me, so I just decided on something that sounded tasty. With great bravado I gave my order to the waiter in what I thought was fluent French. I had practiced the request for the chosen entrée in French under my breath before speaking. The waiter looked at me with a question mark on his face and said "De quel pays êtes-vous?" This perplexed me somewhat; had I not ordered my dish from the menu in fluent French?

"Je me suis Canadian," I responded, "pour quoi? [Why?] Je ne compra pas ce que vous de mander." I understood then that I was not quite as fluent as I thought and, rather than repeat the order in French, I decided to point my finger at the menu for the desired dish. So much for my fluency in French! (But the food tasted very good.)

It was time to move on, in the direction of Tours and Toulouse, further south. I don't remember why I wanted to visit Toulouse. I must have read something about the place that interested me. I arrived at the train station which was, as usual, close to the center of town. I liked the fact that one does not need to take a taxi when traveling with a moderately-sized backpack, but can simply shoulder it walk the streets to look for accommodation. Finding some, one leaves one's baggage there, freeing oneself to browse the streets, parks and whatever takes one's fancy.

I am not a person who spends much time in museums. Instead, I look for opportunities to meet people and get a feel of a their culture. Therefore, I stepped into a pub to try one of France's noted drinks, called a "Pernod"—a greenish liquor. Walking down the darkened streets to my chosen bistro that evening I had to pass some scantily-dressed women. They let me pass. It was not the culture I intended to study.

Arriving at this particular café-bar, the bartender (who happened to be the proprietor) greeted me with "Bonjour, Monsieur, vous desirez?"

My practiced response was, "Donne-moi un Pernod si vous pleit."

He understood me instantly. Finally, I had found my French tongue; my linguistic skills had not left me. He filled a medium-sized glass with that liqueur with a "Voilà, Monsieur". Good, I thought, he understands me perfectly. Maybe we can have a conversation and I can learn something about the local culture. Instead, he asked if I played checkers.

"Not really," I replied.

"Il est très simple," he replied, and brought the checker board unto the bar. He set up a row of checkers on my side of the board with a single checker on the other side, by which he would try to penetrate my single line of defence. He made three attempts and lost. Then he suggested we try one more time and he would bet me a whisky. I was confident that I could win and agreed, but in no time flat he broke through my defence and I lost the bet, fait accomplit, as the French say. When I questioned him about the bill, which seemed a bit high, he replied, "Deux whisky" (a double one). All right, I thought, strike it up to your French cultural experience. Before he sauntered off with a big cigar, and his double whisky to join some of his cronies for chess, he told his bar assistant to keep filling my glass with the local white wine, "Vin de la Pays", as I desired. Deciding I should get full value for my dollars spent there, I made a sizable dent in that bottle at the bar. Though not drunk, I felt no pain, and was rather light-footed—just short of singing—on my way back to the hotel.

Next morning, not totally clear-headed yet, I made my way back to the railway station to check on schedules and directions. The holder of a Euro-rail Pass can go any direction at any time on any train stopping at the station. It's all up to the holder where to go and when. As I said before, my pass was good for three weeks. While checking schedules, two young American students noticed me reading French Pamphlets. Also noting the Canadian badge on my backpack, they assumed I was bilingual and could be of help to them. Feeling respected now as an older, travel-wise person with "language skills", I was glad to be of help, hoping to regain my confidence from the past days' humbling experiences. The two students proposed the idea of heading for Spain. I thought it a good idea and agreed to join them, since they both liked the idea of having a bilingual Canadian along. We checked train schedules and were on our way. After crossing into Spain, we met an English gentleman, familiar with the country, who suggested a place called "Palamos", near Barcelona, where there was a great holiday resort with a nice beach. We disembarked at the station and took a taxi to a small, old hotel, just a few kilometres away. We were put up in one room with three beds for $5 each.

It was 3 p.m. We put on our swimming gear and headed for the beach just a few blocks away. The thirty-degree Celsius temperature was perfect. Sitting on the beach, we shared our different backgrounds. They were both college students: one from New York, the other, Florida. They were slated to attend a foreign culture and language course in Germany in a few weeks.

That evening, we dined in a nice restaurant by the sea and splurged on a glass of Spanish wine. The bottle cost more than their total daily budget of $25. I was glad to have more resources than they, as well as a credit card for back up.

Next day, being an early riser, I strolled into town for a continental breakfast. Then I proceeded to walk along the cobbled, main shopping street which sloped down towards the waterfront. Suddenly I spied a shop with a door curtain of wooden beads strung vertically. For lack of a better word I name it a bead curtain. Immediately I realized it would fit perfectly as a divider between our family room and the hallway in our home—which had Spanish-style architecture—in Edmonton. Unfortunately, the elderly woman in the shop was not selling bead curtains and did not speak English or French. I resorted to hand signals to ask where I could obtain one. She pointed down the street and, sure enough, I found the place. Eureka: curtains made of beads on strings! The proprietor told me they could custom-make them according to specific measurements. The condition was, I had to prepay in cash. However, they would not ship it to the address of one of my brothers in Holland. What to do? A bead curtain was heavy and awkward to carry, yet I was determined to have one. I said I would be back later and left the shop. I went to the beach and walked up and down along the beach until I heard Dutch spoken. Here was a family vacationing and returning to Holland in a few days. I asked if they could transport my curtain back to Holland and drop it off at my brother's place for a fee. They agreed, providing no drugs were involved. I assured them there weren't and we mad a deal. I rushed back to the shop, told them to make it ready and paid the agreed price in cash. The next morning I delivered it to the Dutch family's apartment and, in due time, it was delivered to my brother's place.

For dinner I joined up with my fellow travelers, the students. Since we had dined at a somewhat upscale place the night before, we decided to eat at our hotel this time. There, for $5 per person, a three course meal could be had, including wine, which was half the price of the previous meal without the wine. And it was delicious.

After two days in Palamos, we returned to France the way we came. Once inside the border, I headed for Avignon, while the other two went the opposite direction to see the Atlantic coast and Bordeaux.

In Avignon, I found a place not far from the railway station and went to bed early. I was tired from traveling on the train, mostly standing up, hoisting a few beers, and sharing and discussing experiences with other tourists of other languages.

At this point in the trip, I found myself with a real need for conversation, wanting to communicate with someone who spoke my language. (I always carry a few paper-back novels with me to keep sane when unable to converse with someone else.) An opportunity presented itself when I was walking in the downtown square. I saw a few people in poor attire sitting on a bench sharing a bottle of wine. When they saw me staring at them, they called me over to join them for a drink. I hesitated for a second, then thought, You are here to study language and culture, so accept the invitation and you will be rewarded with a new experience, if not a new attitude. Well, it took only one sip of that cheap wine to convince me to keep the conversation was very short. With a "Merci bien" I took off.

In the 16th century, Avignon was where the alternate pope lived, in competition with the one in Rome, in a Magnificent Palace called, "Palais du Pap", adjacent to the Rhone River. Originally, a bridge spanning the river had been constructed, but it had later been partially destroyed and not repaired. Interested in this bit of history, I looked for a tour guide who spoke English. Failing to find one, I followed the French one, then started again with a German-speaking guide, thinking that whatever I might have missed on the first tour, I could pick up on the second. I liked the city of Avignon, but it was time to move on; I had a long itinerary.

I avoided large cities where one feels like a needle in a haystack; I felt they were not conducive to meeting people on a one-to-one basis. For my next stop I choose a small resort town called, "Beaulieu sur la Mer" just short of Nice. It was a place I could go for a jog and a swim. The beach, in mid-afternoon, was not busy. I saw a topless woman sunbathing. Somehow, that made me feel less conspicuous going out for a swim myself. It was a wonderful day, with exercise, rest, and a splendid view from my small hostel up the hill, overlooking the Mediterranean Sea and its surrounding natural beauty.

The next morning, I got on the train for Monaco, location of the renowned residence of Prince Rainier and Princess Grace Kelly. Upon my arrival I had breakfast, consisting of an omelette with toast and coffee. (I had missed this in France where the usual breakfast consisted of croissants or baguettes with butter and jam.) Next, I wandered around the principality, admiring the luxurious palace. But the folks there made no balcony appearance to greet me.

Back on the train, I headed for Italy. The train followed the Mediterranean coastline where, from time to time, the sea was visible. We passed the town of Pisa, known for its leaning tower. Not interested in having it lean on me, I opted to pass it by to give me more time to spend in "Firenza" (Florence). Florence is a city rich in renaissance history, where, during the 16th century, the Medici family ruled. During the renaissance period many palaces and cathedrals were built, with their interiors full of paintings and sculptures.

I spent three days in Florence enjoying the visual reminders of its past, absorbing its splendour and meditating on its former significance as a strategic centre of power. I had heard about a small, ancient place called "Fiesole", situated some 8 km outside the city and at a considerably higher elevation. It was a stronghold where, more than 1000 years ago, the ruling tribes of Tuscany had lived. During its heyday, the Etrusco tribe was in power. I took a bus up a long, winding road to view the ruins of Fiesole, including an amphitheatre.

Before leaving that morning, I was wearing my running shoes, a pair of shorts and a T-shirt, because I intended to get my exercise by running back down to Florence along that sometimes steep, winding road. When I left Fiesole at about 12:30 p.m., I took of my T-shirt to keep it from getting soaked in sweat; already the temperature was nearing 30 degrees Celsius. I ran at an easy pace, until the downward road became steeper and I automatically increased my speed. It was getting pretty hot; the perspiration was running down my face and chest. Reaching the city limits, I was looking for a sign saying "City Centre". From there I would look for signs saying Railway Station or "STAZIONE" and then I would be able to locate my hostel. All went well until I reached the city centre where no signs of "stazione" appeared. I began to ask people on the sidewalk for directions, by repeating the word "stazione". It was getting close to siesta time by then; shops were closing as I was running along the sidewalk. With my face deep red, my hair matted, and sweat pouring down my face and chest, I must have looked a bit freaky. Just then a well-dressed woman came out of a shop. I repeated the word "STAZIONE, STAZIONE" and waved my arm in a half circle to indicate what direction I should take. The woman just let out a screech and rushed back into the shop.

Sorry!

Somehow I managed to find my way back to my hostel. I showered and rested and wondered what was to come next. From the loss of body fluid during my downhill run, my legs got stiff and remained cramped for more than a week.

My next destination was Rome. I did not enjoy my few days there; partly it was my own fault. Usually, I can find my way around with a road map and pamphlets, but the method failed me this time. I should have taken a guided tour of the city. I missed some places of interest that might have given me a more positive feeling about this historical place, Rome. I started by taking a bus to St. Peter's Square. I went into St. Peter's Cathedral, which I found majestic and impressive. Here one can admire sculptures and paintings done by Michael Angelo and others. In the great, open sanctuary I observed a half dozen priests giving communion to tourists, each giving the sacrament in different languages to suit the tourists' needs. I presumed this was how they raised donations for the upkeep of the cathedral. Personally, I did not find the majesty of Christianity in that cathedral; neither did I see it as a warm place to worship and have fellowship. Actually, I found it somewhat intimidating. I felt the same way in similar large cathedrals; the brick and mortar, sculpture and paintings made me feel I had to kneel for its splendour, not so much in worship to God. Perhaps other tourists felt blessed by this experience, I do not know. I walked back to my hostel via a large boulevard to see the

"Fountana di Trivi" and other noteworthy places. The next day I viewed the coliseum, which was very dilapidated—not attractive to the eye. I looked forward taking the train to Brindisi, from where I would take the boat to Corfu and Athens, Greece. From there I had planned to fly back to Amsterdam, then home to Canada.

Before boarding the train in Rome I went across the train station for some pizza and beer. As I stood outside the station with my backpack eating my pizza, a couple of young kids approached me for a handout. A panhandler a hundred feet away alerted me that they were pick-pockets. Not knowing the suitable Italian words, I told them to get lost by pretending to kick them. I was not aware that it was too late.

The train was packed with summer travelers and I was lucky to find a seat in the first class coach. It took the conductor about an hour before he reached our coach to check out tickets, or in my case, the Euro-rail pass. Reaching for my wallet, I discovered it was not in the usual pocket or in any other pocket. I had lost it; the pick-pockets had got the better of me. At this point, the conductor was too busy with other passengers in the crowded train to worry about it. I knew I would have to get off the train and return to Rome and Holland because my credit cards were also missing, besides some hard cash. I did have my passport and some traveler's cheques in a hidden pocket for such an emergency, so I was not immediately worried. Checking my map, I saw the next major stop would be Benevento. There, I left the train.

I decided to contact the railway police to report the theft, but they sent for the city police who picked me up and took me to their main station. The city police proceeded to write a report of my lost belongings, with French as the medium to communicate. As their French was no better than mine, they decided to call an interpreter, who was a school teacher. Thus, it did not take very long to have a report completed, showing a list of articles lost. I put the report in my wallet and pocketed it.

As I left the police station and headed back toward the train depot, I admittedly felt very disappointed at having to curtail my travel plans. At the same time, I was glad to have a report of my stolen wallet and its contents. If nothing else, it would serve as a souvenir. However, I planned to use this report to my advantage. Optimistically, I saw it as a way to convince the next conductor that I was robbed of my pass. Perhaps, I reasoned, he would have compassion on me and let me ride the train for free.

Just then, two young people wearing backpacks passed me. As I turned to take a second look, they did likewise. We smiled at one another and struck up a conversation. I learned that they were college students from the States who were taking Italian language courses in Italy. They confessed that they were pretending to be broke and hoped to hitchhike to Sorrento on the coast. They had already spoken to a train station employee who offered them a ride to an other station some distance away. From there they could get a train to Solerno, the nearest town to Sorrento. They invited me to join them, and I heartily agreed. Their contact person at the station agreed to accommodate me but did so grudgingly. My two new, student friends were female, which was likely the reason he drove his car very fast and said little.

We arrived at the station in time to catch the train to Solerno. Disembarking at our destination, two handsome-looking Italian men offered us a ride. Convinced it would save time, we hopped into their car and drove along the beautiful, winding coastline, crowded with cars. We drank in the scenery and stopped to watch the sun recede into the Gulf of Naples. Arriving in Sorrento we could see the Island of Capri not far off.

I realized these two students didn't need this old fart's protection and were probably more street-wise than me. They were probably relieved when I suggested we part company. I registered in a hostel, showered and went to bed.

I arose early to take the bus back to Solerno, from where I took the train towards Rome. Once there, I intended to register and cancel my two credit cards. Since I did not have my rail pass anymore, I developed a game plan to get back to Holland in the first class section of the train. When boarding the trains, I would look for compartments with people who appeared friendly. I would engage them in conversation, hoping we at least had one language in common. I would then explain my predicament of being robbed of my wallet, money and rail-pass, and would show them my police report for confirmation. Then I would show it to the conductor when he came around. This way, I speculated, while the conductor was reading the police report, the eyes of my fellow passengers would be on him, not on me. I would then throw up my hands in misery, hoping he would let me go. Using this convincing strategy with the conductors, I managed to get a free ride part of the way back to Holland.

I altered my subterfuge at the Swiss border, however. There, the conductors speak two or three languages and are not easily taken in. When the train stopped there, I got off to meet the new conductor before boarding his train. I explained my predicament and, again, showed my police report. I suggested that when he reached my compartment, where fellow travelers could be observing, I would show him some document that could pass for a rail pass. After some hesitation he agreed, provided I get off in Lucerne; there a different conductor would board who could cause him embarrassment. I readily agreed, because I was exhausted anyway.

Lucerne is a beautiful city nestled in the mountains. I hoped to spend two nights there, but the weather changed to rain by mid-day, and I decided to head for home. Maybe someday I would come back with my wife, who would enjoy this place for its splendid views.

Leaving Lucerne, the conductor showed up, but did not check my pass.

In Basil, the border city into Germany, a new conductor checked our tickets. That's when I got into trouble; my game was up. This conductor was not moved by a police report and a back-packer gesticulating with agonized expressions. No amount of explanation, no excuses or pleading would persuade him to allow me to ride his train in the first class compartment beyond the next stop, Karlsruhe. I simply had to get off. With no more tricks up my sleeve, I knew the free ride was over. I had come a long way, though, I reasoned; indeed, I had almost made it, and I was not disappointed. After all, my interrupted travel had had an exciting end!

After the conductor saw me off in Karlsruhe, I cashed one of my traveler's cheques that I had hidden in my money belt. I entered the train station and bought a ticket in second class to Amsterdam. It was not demeaning. In fact, I had a lot of fun with some black American soldiers who were, like me, in a holiday mood. I even considered the idea of attending a dance with them, but was led to say, "No." Francis, I thought, it is time to go home.

It was 11 p.m. when I arrived in Amsterdam. I stayed the night and, the next morning, met my relatives in Andijk, who were eager to hear about my adventures. A few days after that, I was back in Canada—my home, sweet home—where Grace welcomed me like her long lost love.

29

TAKING A SABBATICAL (1983)

I was always kind of envious of pastors and university professors going on sabbaticals. Why do business people not take sabbaticals? I wondered. Don't they deserve a break from their tedious or stressful work?

I certainly felt I could use a break. I was doing well as a life insurance representative and often received praise for my efforts. While this was encouraging, it also put pressure on me to do better, to increase my production, or, simply put, to make more money. I began to agree with the saying, "You cannot live by bread alone".

On a few occasions during workday hours, while walking towards the underground parking area of our office tower, I felt drawn to a restaurant bar, located nearby. Of course, going for a drink after work would have been fine; I often have one at home. But it struck me as odd, and perhaps a bit dangerous, that in mid-afternoon I was drawn to stop in for a drink, without company. I realized that I needed to unwind, but it worried me. If I needed to unwind, why couldn't I wait until I was at home? I was concerned that if I stopped at a bar one time, it might become a habit; it might result in my becoming enslaved to alcohol. Is this how some people develop a problem with alcohol?

I came to the conclusion that praise could shorten a person's lifespan. It would be better to enjoy more time with family and to smell the roses in my own back yard. Perhaps it was time for a "sabbatical"! I had already taken correspondence courses at Athabasca University, before switching to the King's University College where I could attend lectures. Now, in my 3rd year and on my way to getting a degree in history, I decided to take a course in Holland.

My dear wife, Grace, was not enthusiastic about us spending four months in Amsterdam, away from our house and family, including a nineteen-year-old daughter at home by herself. Also, when my manager found out, a few months before Grace and I left for Amsterdam, he went ballistic. He had just finished his report for the head office, with his production expectations for the New Year. "Oh, no!" he said, "You cannot do that!" I told him yes, I could do that and reminded him that I had mentioned it to him several years before. I said that I wanted to study history and stressed that I needed a break from the routine. We argued and threats were made, but he realized my mind was made up. In the end, while concerned about financial implications for the company, he was concerned for me as well and accepted it. So, we worked it out. My part was to arrange for other agents to look after my clients.

Having freed ourselves up, Grace and I joined a group of students from Dordt College, Iowa, who were going to Amsterdam in January, 1983, to study art and architecture, language, culture and history. I had applied to join them and had been accepted.

The young folks stayed in a student dormitory while the two of us managed to rent half an apartment next to a park. With the climate of Holland being much milder than that of Canada, we knew that the first flowers would be in evidence there by March. The "free" university was within walking distance. For Grace, there were many shops of interest. She loved the idea of going for a walk and picking up just enough groceries for the day. Flowers were inexpensive and we always had a fresh bouquet in our small sitting room. There were a wide variety of colourful tulips, chrysanthemums, carnations, roses, etc. We were fortunate to be able to rent a small, used BMW from a nephew who could not afford to drive it. We were both happy. We felt rich, able to drive around the country to meet up with our Dutch siblings on weekends, hoping to be asked for dinner and gladly accepting in exchange for flowers. Our youngest daughter, Marianne, still single, also came to visit for a week before we returned to Canada.

Some of my courses required visiting parts of old cities and taking a close look at the different architectural designs from the sixteen to the twentieth centuries. As we walked through the inner section of the cities, some streets were cobblestone, and streetcars on rails rumbled by.

In studying Dutch history, we were taken to different museums. In both cases, Grace was allowed to come along. So it was that we revisited, with great interest, the culture we had left behind so many years before when we emigrated.

We had a wonderful time, apart from dealing with our landlady. We were required to share the kitchen with the old lady who had rented us a bed/sitting room in her apartment on the sixth floor. This woman was very frugal—in the common vernacular, a real "cheapskate". All in all, though, it was a great experience, and I got five credits toward my college degree.

Arriving back in Edmonton, we were welcomed back by our daughter to our comfortable home. Grace was happy to be back in her private domain. As for me, with my head still full of the recent excitement, I had to get back on track. Contacting my clientele, I found they had not missed me. No one had planned to die in my absence; all were alive and well.

Still, back at work on the first of June, I had a terrible time getting into the swing of it.

I needed to get into the right routine: analyzing a prospective customer's needs, following up with a suitable presentation, etc. Thankfully, things got back to normal and I reached my production objective for the year. My manager was happy to see us back and to see me resuming my normal routine, which increased his own production goals for the year.

Our finances, then, were still intact. We were not broke(n), just badly dented. It was worth it!

30

RUNNING THE MARATHON

It was the last day of February, 1971, in the town of Seaside, Oregon, that I ran my first marathon. It was 26 miles and 385 yards, or 42 km.

The story begins with me joining the YMCA and entering the *Keep Fit* exercise program. Three times a week our class met, and on the in-between days I swam.

I wasn't in very good shape when I joined the YMCA in 1967. My career as a life insurance agent was too sedentary; I wasn't getting enough exercise. I had "softened up" you might say. My weight had increased to where I was showing a bulge in my midriff, and my muscles had become flabby. A man could loose his self-respect!

The *Keep Fit* classes had become a necessity and I attended faithfully. Soon my sagging profile tightened up, my lung capacity increased and my heart rate came down. All in all this man began to take pride in his body and physique.

After about one year of classes we were introduced to the benefits of jogging and running. A book written by a Major Cooper, an ex-doctor in the U. S. Air Force had done some research and had kept statistics about different types of exercises. He'd made interesting comparisons on expended energy within a specific time frame for each type of sport: swimming, cycling, running, etc. Running became the "in thing" in those days. It brought quick results because of its intensity.

Being a restless person by nature, it was just what I needed. After a few weeks of training with my class, I could outrun them all in both time and distance. I hadn't known I had it in me. In my younger days, playing in soccer games, I had always chosen to be the linesman. All I had to do was to run along the edge of the field holding the flag and waving it when the ball was out of bounds.

Realizing I had a natural ability to run, I entered some competitions. I was impressed with myself. I hadn't known people could run such long distances, let alone that I could. I had been good at high jumping in my youth but had never done distance running.

When a person does well in a sport he gets praised. The praise I received did a lot for my ego and consequently I trained even harder. Someone suggested I enter the Journal 5-mile Road Race in May, 1969. I finished first in my age class. The additional praise fuelled my ambition to achieve greater goals.

It was then that Bill Bannister came on the scene with the idea of running a marathon. I didn't know what a marathon was. When Bill explained, I said, "You must be crazy, Bill, a horse can't run that far!" "Well," said Bill, "it's not that difficult; it's just a matter of training." I thought, Oh yeah?

Of course, my ego was stroked. I fell for the idea and we started training, running longer distances. Weekdays at noon, we would run, alternating 5 km runs at a fast tempo with 10 km runs at an easier pace. On Saturdays, we did distances of 15 and 25 km to build stamina. Speed was not important in the beginning of this training. We would run at an 8-minute-mile pace (we were not yet fully in the metric system), and the shorter ones a half minute per mile faster.

Since our marathon race was not until the end of February, we needed to keep training during the winter. Because of the snow on the roads, I would go to Hawrelak Park, which was ploughed, and would run circles around it. We had a dog at the time, named Seal. I took him along one time. At first he ran ahead of me and jumped over the snow banks on the side of the road, sniffing for scents. After about 10 km, however, he slowed considerably, and by the 15-km mark he was completely tuckered out.

Our objective was to run at least three 15-mile distance-training runs before leaving for Oregon. When the day arrived for our travel to Seaside, we teamed up with some runner friends in Calgary. We drove the distance in a day and a night. There was one more night before the race, so we turned in early to be fresh the next morning at 10:00 am.

We stayed at an older hotel next to the start and finish line of the race. It was an inexpensive hotel, the cost commensurate with most of the athletes' ability to pay. Our breakfast consisted of pancakes with syrup, the type of breakfast favoured because it is light and easy to digest.

Lining up the following morning, about five hundred runners were milling around. Everybody had already run a few miles for warm-up and had emptied their bowels to get ready for the starting gun.

Since five hundred runners can't all be in the front row, we lined up according to our ability and speed. The line was about half a block long. Since I always have high expectations of myself I placed myself close to the front. Bill was with me.

When the gun went off, the stampede of runners behind us nearly trampled us. As a result, we made a fast start, less than 7 minutes in the first mile. "Too fast," Bill said, "We won't last at that speed." Bill and I had made a pact to run together from start to finish.

It was a cold morning, about 42°F (6°C). The roads were wet from some snow and rain which had fallen during the night. Just the same, we wore shorts and T-shirts. A few runners added toques and mittens. The sun peeked through the clouds, at times, and brought the temperature to 45 degrees.

We made good progress and were pleased to note, at mile ten, that we were running ahead of schedule. There were water stations every 5 miles, as it was important to drink whether feeling thirsty or not. It is surprising how much fluid a body loses through perspiration.

We checked our time again at the 15-mile mark and our progress averaged about 7¾ minutes per mile. We felt encouraged; so far so good.

At the 18-mile point we were expecting to "hit the wall". Hitting the wall is an expression for a condition in which the glucose, or blood sugar, in the body is depleted. With this source of energy used up, the body begins to draw energy from stored fat. To convert the fat into energy requires a physiological changeover. Since we had not trained beyond the 18-mile distance we had not experienced this and wondered when it would happen. We did not have long to wait. It started at the 20-mile mark and became increasingly debilitating. I started to feel a void under my rib cage, an emptiness that made me want desperately to quit running. Bill said, "Just keep it up. Ignore the feeling. You can do it."

By this time, we passed several runners who were walking; they had run too fast in the beginning. It would have been the same for me had Bill not slowed me down.

We were now nearing the end. In those last miles, people were cheering us on. With blurry eyes I saw a young woman in a T-shirt with Heineken Beer emblazoned across the chest. I wanted, as usual, to drool but had no saliva left.

So on I went. Fortunately, the running surface was mostly flat at this point; the slightest rise was pure agony. With a mile to go, Bill spurred me on to make a dash for the finish line, but I was near collapse, my eyes starting to glaze over.

With about a hundred yards to go Bill took my hand and we sped past the finish line into the arms of our comrades who had finished more than a half hour ago. We had competed the race in 3 hours and 26 minutes, just under the 8-minute per mile objective.

After some minutes of rest and revival—walking, easing up from the run—we went to our rooms for showers and rest. The trouble for me was that my room was on the third floor and there were no elevators; I had to climb the stairs. I did this by holding onto and pulling myself up by the handrails. When I got to my room I had no key to get in. I had left it at the desk downstairs before the run, since I had no pocket to put it in. Now what to do? I looked for a chambermaid to help me out, but saw no one. There was no way out but to go down the stairs again. Fortunately, there was a maid on the second floor, and she let me back into my room. I pleaded for her to run my bath, which she did, becoming concerned for my wellbeing. There was nothing more she could do, short of helping me into the tub, which was not offered.

After a half hour of lounging I hoisted myself, still stiff, out of the tub. I dried myself and drank more liquids, including some apple cider with low alcohol content. I dozed on the bed for an hour. A few more swallows of cider helped revive me sufficiently to walk over to the school gymnasium where race results were to be announced. We were fed pork and beans with coleslaw. My stomach was not quite ready to digest it yet, so I ate sparingly.

We left Seaside that evening about 9 pm. The person in our car who was not a runner drove the first stretch. I sat in the back seat, finished the apple cider and managed to slumber for a few hours. By early morning, I was sober and relaxed enough to take the wheel for a while. We arrived in Calgary the next evening and I stayed in a hotel for the night before traveling on to Edmonton.

A year later, in 1972, I ran the same course, without Bill this time, and finished the race in 3 hours, 3 minutes (averaging 7 miles per minute). Three months later, at age 43, I finished the Journal 5-mile Road Race in 26:44 minutes, an average pace of 5:21 min. per mile. I finished first in my age class, and 16th over all out of a hundred runners.

The last marathon I ran was in 1981. By this time, however, my right knee was becoming painful from running, so I gave it up and took up cycling instead.

31

JOSEPH

One Sunday morning our pastor led us in worship with a sermon entitled, "Did you see God leading?" It was about the Biblical story of Joseph, Jacob's son. Jacob showed more love toward Joseph than he did toward his other sons. This resulted in jealousy from the older boys toward their younger brother, and they despised him. Their dislike was so great that when Joseph came to visit them in a far-off part of their property where they were herding their flock, they decided to sell him to a trader. Joseph ended up in Egypt where he eventually became the most trusted administrator of the kingdom.

Something in this story struck me as familiar. My two older brothers, in jest, called me Joseph sometimes. Perhaps it had to do with our seating arrangement at the family dining table when I was growing up. My place was next to my father. Left of me sat my brother Herman and opposite me, my brother Jan. My Dad and brothers would talk shop. I, who was about 10-12 years old and needed to be under close supervision because of my restless energy, would interrupt their conversation. I was bored and wanted to get away from the dining table to play, but I was not allowed to leave the table until after the meal when devotions were completed. The extra attention I got from my father was the reason, I think, that they called me Joseph. I was not very happy with this name, but I had to live with it.

My dad was always concerned about me because I was apt to get into trouble one way or another. When my mother could not handle a situation, I was referred to my father to be dealt with. He would always hear me out like a judge, and then decide what action to take: hands on my backside or shut into a room to think over my misbehaviour.

When I reached the age of adolescence I had to share the work in the field, crawling on my knees in the dirt and pulling weeds, or worse, digging up tulip bulbs or potatoes, which I found very tiresome and boring. I would try feigning a stomach-ache or find some other excuse. Gradually, after working with other field hands that had no protecting father, I realized I had to smarten up and show I could do my share.

In the early (nineteen) forties we acquired a horse to modernize our field work with mechanical implements. That's were I blossomed. I loved to work with this heavy workhorse. I would harness him and ride him bareback to the field. On a few occasions, when the horse was not needed and was resting in the stable, I went galloping around the village, which scared the wits out of some elderly ladies.

When I turned 18, I was to be conscripted into the army. My cousin Pete and I discussed what this would mean for our future. At the time, Holland was trying to reclaim Indonesia from the Japanese occupation but the natives were opposed to the idea. We knew that serving there would take two to three years of our youth, possibly causing us to miss out on other interesting opportunities.

We had uncles and cousins that had immigrated to Canada before the Second World War and we asked our parents for consent to go and start a new life there. My father, who had visited his brothers and had seen Canada and loved it, concurred with the idea. Consequently, I and two other cousins immigrated to Canada in April 1948.

In hindsight, it appears I truly was my father's Joseph after all. He realized that if I, with my temperament, had become a soldier, I might have done something foolish and gotten myself killed.

Over the next forty years, I worked as a farmhand, a sawmill worker, an assistant agent for the Canadian National Railway, and a representative of a seed company until, finally, I was recruited by a life insurance company in 1959.

In 1987, I became a below-knee amputee (left side) due to an accident while riding my bicycle. I was laid up for nearly three years due to complications in a number of surgeries.

From that point on, I had a lot of time to reflect on my past. I started thinking about what God had in store for me. I never questioned God why I should be disabled. I could accept it as my due. Things happened to others, I reasoned; why should I be spared? We live in broken world, and I am no better than anyone else. However, I did feel that God was by my side all the way, as before and ever since. I believe He loves me, and I want to be his servant.

I was always a staunch believer, trying to live as a Christian by following the do's and don'ts. My prayers were sincere, but I was not asking God to steer me in the right direction. I did serve as a deacon or an elder several times, both as a duty and with enjoyment. I was a good listener, which is half the battle in helping people getting rid of their frustration or worries about sickness or death.

After my accident, I managed quite well, physically, despite my handicap. It was my prayer life that changed the most. I began seeking what God had in store for me. I started to reflect on my past. What was God telling me? This is where my Joseph complex came to the forefront.

Incidentally, I had taken up a new hobby as a Ham radio operator. I had to have call sign that required three initials of my name. Not having a middle name, I was short a letter and added a middle letter "J" to become "FJR", as in Foxtrot Joseph Romeo. I liked it; it sounded grand to me and somewhat reminiscent of my past. (Actually the complete call sign was VE6-FJR and was properly expressed as Victor Echo Six Foxtrot Julia Romeo.)

I often went over my past. Reflecting on the times I had traveled by myself and had gotten into situations that might have led me astray, I became aware that God had prevented me from going astray a number of times. It was as if angels had botched my attempts to associate with the wrong crowd. I have always been able to face my family and friends with a clean heart. For this I have forever been thankful.

Yes, I pondered the Joseph complex often in recent years. God has been with me all the time. I have become more aware that he owns me.

Although I was slow to accept volunteer work, I prayed that God would use me in some way to honour Him. I know He does not need me—He has all kinds of helpers—but I declared my willingness to serve Him in some capacity.

Now I think I have found it. Here in our senior citizens' home, I read Biblical stories and I read stories about myself that tell people who I am. I try to be kind to the elderly who feel lonely. Yes, I believe God is giving me direction; I accept it with thanksgiving.

32

HITCHHIKING SWEDEN (1979)

While I was visiting my birthplace in Holland, my brother Herman suggested I join him on a business trip to Denmark and Sweden. We made a few stops in Denmark and, the following day, took a ferry to Sweden and stayed overnight in the town of Hasslehome.

I got up early the next morning, six a.m., to seek out a running trail recommended to me by some young people whom I had met in a pub the night before. I found the park and a path and started to run. After going for about twenty minutes in one direction, I turned around to head back to the hotel. On my return, however, I noticed a fork in the trail and I took the way that seemed to be a short cut back to town. Although I had checked the direction of the sun's rays to ensure that I was on the right track, I was led astray. After running a few minutes, I came up to a fence. I kept running along even though the territory was now unfamiliar to me. Following the fence, I came to a large gate with a sign indicating an army base.

What to do?

I saw no one to ask for direction, so I kept running and keeping left, thinking this would take me back onto the right track. Instead, it led through a shooting range. (Thankfully no shots were fired.) By now, I was really getting worried.

Finally, I met a farmer and asked for help. He did not understand English or German or Dutch, but I kept repeating the name of the town and waving my arms with a questioning gesture as to which way I should go. He got the message and pointed whence I came.

By running back through the shooting gallery, I got back to the gravel road and the army entrance. Just then, I saw an army truck in a cloud of dust coming in my direction. I decided to stand on the middle of the road and wave my arms to make it stop.

It did, but the driver was not pleased and looked at me with scowling eyes. He, too, spoke no English, but I showed him a map, from the hotel, of the town and its surrounding area. He looked at it and pointed, indicating that I was beyond the scope of the map. To get to Hasslehome, he pointed out, I had to continue on this gravel road until I reached a highway.

I was getting tired by this time and wondered how far I still had to go. The answer came when, at the highway, there was a sign indicating 5 km to Hasslehome.

Time was running out, because my brother and I needed to catch the ferry at a certain time for our return trip. Attempting to hitchhike, I stuck out my thumb, but to no avail. On impulse, I pretended to be hurting and started to walk with a pronounced limp. Sure enough, a pickup truck driver stopped and gave me a ride to the outskirts of Hasslehome and let me out. I said, "Danke, danke" and ran to my hotel. I did not look back to see the driver's face and whether or not he noticed me running limp-free and realized I tricked him.

After a one-minute shower and change of clothes, I ran downstairs where breakfast was served and where my brother was, anxious for me turn up. I grabbed a glass of milk and a few buns and off we went, getting to the ferry just in time, the last vehicle to get on board.

33

HITCHHIKING QUEEN CHARLOTTE ISLAND

In April 1984, I needed a break after three months' intensive work selling life insurance for Canada Life. The year before, I had taken a four-month sabbatical to study history, language and literature in the Netherlands. I needed to recoup some of my lost income for that period, so I put a lot of pressure on myself to get as much work as possible done before the summer arrived with its slower sales. However this intensive activity resulted in abdominal pain, diagnosed as an inflammation of the intestines. I'd had this experience before and knew I had to take a break, try to relax, watch my diet and do light exercises. Also the thought struck me that I could test myself to see how I would endure an adventure with some inconveniences.

Since I am action oriented I stuffed my backpack with a tent, a sleeping bag and other accoutrements and took a train to Prince Rupert on the Pacific coast for a week's outing. From there I took a flight to the Queen Charlotte Islands on an amphibious plane, nicknamed "The Flying Goose". (The ferry was not in service due to stormy weather.)

I walked through the town of Queen Charlotte looking for a place to put up my tent in a park or campsite. I met some people who offered to let me stay in their automobile and I was happy to accept their offer. Then, however, I noticed dark clouds were coming in and I knew that camping would not be good. I opted for a cheap hotel, instead, for $20.00

a night. This proved fortunate, because it rained bucketsful all night with winds of up to 100 km an hour.

The following two days I made excursions around the island and enjoyed the sights of the Haida Indian Nation. I had a chance meeting with two other tourists who invited me to join them in sight seeing.

On the third day I took the ferry back to the mainland. I found out that, after arriving at the harbour of Prince Rupert, there would be no transportation to Edmonton by train or bus for at least 6 hours. Instead of sitting and waiting around for the next bus I decided to try to hitchhike my way home.

While the ferryboat steamed towards Prince Rupert I walked around the decks, making conversation with whomever I could engage. Soon I found a woman, a permanent resident of the island, traveling by car in my direction. I explained that I had no transportation from Prince Rupert to my cousin's place in Houston, a two-hundred-mile distance.

"Oh," she said, "I would be most happy to give you a ride, because I find it boring to drive by myself". She accepted me as someone who could appreciate the life and beauty on the islands. I suppose that made me trustworthy in her eyes.

I arrived in Houston about 10 p.m. and stayed overnight with my cousin. Continuing on my way the following morning, I had only walked about half a mile when a pickup truck stopped and a young fellow offered me a ride. He was from Idaho and said he could drop me off in Prince George, about another two hundred miles further on.

Arriving in Prince George I suggested we have a bite to eat. He welcomed the idea and we enjoyed the meal. I picked up the bill and took it to the cashier, pulling out my American Express Gold Card. You should have seen his face! Not only was I able to pay for the food, but I had this classy credit card to use for payment. His thinking changed; instead of having reservations about me, thinking this scruffy-looking hitchhiker was probably down and out, he saw me as his equal. He was so impressed that he gave me his home address and invited me to his place any time I was in the vicinity.

He dropped me off at the city limits of Prince George. By this time it was after five o'clock in the afternoon. I had been so fortunate with this trip that I thought I must be a master in hitchhiking.

Wrong thought!

I started walking and thumbing along the highway with no success. After walking for three miles, someone gave me a lift for five miles, and then I walked and thumbed again. On and on I walked, with hardly any other traffic. At dusk, walking up a long hill, I saw a farmhouse not far off the road and wondered whether I should knock on their door and see if they would take me in. I began to think that I was stupid not to have stayed overnight in Prince George. As I looked to see where I could put up my tent, I saw snow under the trees along the highway, and knew this was not a good place.

In the meantime it got completely dark and I despaired. I felt I was in deep trouble and would have to use some unorthodox way to get someone to stop. When the next vehicle came over the hill traveling at low speed, I ran out waving both arms and looking frantic. Lo and behold, they stopped!

It was a worn bit of a pickup truck with two innocuous-looking young fellows sitting in the cab. They asked what my problem was and I explained my dilemma. They took pity on me and invited me to come on board. I threw my backpack in the back of the truck amidst some other junk, and sat between the two of them in the front seat. Off we went. They traveled fairly slowly, explaining that the front brakes were not working, and one of their gears was inoperable. Well, I reasoned, I am cozy inside, we are going in the right direction, and I have no other choice.

Continuing on their journey they pulled some cans of beer from behind the seat and I realized they had downed a number of them already. They offered me one, too. I reasoned that if I drank some of their beer they might run out, keeping them half-way sober. Besides, as a tired old man (55) who was down on his luck, I could stand a beer anyway. Actually, memories came back to me from 1950 of being a bushwhacker in a 1936 Buick coupe, having consumed "a few for the road" and feeling no pain. Therefore I was in somewhat familiar company.

Things went well. They behaved and kept at a low speed. I felt comforted; the beer was all gone and we should arrive safely at the Tete Jaune Junction, from where they would go south and I would continue eastward.

This was not to be. After traveling more than an hour at 75 km/hr through winding and hilly territory, not seeing a soul, they decided to stop in McBride, a small town that had a beer parlour. I felt dismayed, but what could I do? As they were my rescuers, I was in no position to argue. I thought they would stop and pick up half a dozen beers and go on. Instead, they took a seat in the bar and ordered several beers. I must admit that I was getting dry, too, and hoisted one with them for good cheer and in appreciation of their charity toward me. After half an hour, satisfied for the time being, they obtained another case of beer for the road. Obviously, they had no intentions of going dry.

I was very relieved when, half an hour later, we arrived at the Tete Jaune junction and they stopped to let me out. As I opened the passenger door, several bottles of beer fell out onto the pavement, the full ones spilling beer on to the road. I hastily thanked my chauffer and benefactor, wishing him a bon voyage. I was grateful to be alive and able-bodied, and I was ready to move on.

By now it was about eleven in the evening. The moon was out, the air was fairly mild, and no frost was expected. I walked up a long steep hill, thinking I might get a ride, but no such luck. Spotting a good place to put up my tent, just off the road, I bedded down, tired and fully clothed, but at peace. No scary dreams followed me, and I had a refreshing slumber.

Early in the morning I was awakened by an air horn blast from a passing truck. He probably thought it was time to rise and shine. I tried to read the time of day on my watch but could not make out what I was looking at until I realized I was still wearing my toque and it had slipped over my eyes. It was 6 a.m.

Folding my tent and sleeping bag, I found some 2-day-old crusts of bread in my backpack, which I was able to swallow with some tepid water from a bottle I carried.

Soon I was back on the road, thumbing, hoping someone would give me a ride in the direction of Jasper and on to Edmonton. After walking and thumbing for half an hour, I got a ride for about 10 miles. From there on, I had no lifts for several hours.

My feet were getting sore; I had forgotten to change socks. I felt forlorn. After an hour's walk, with my pack feeling heavier, I was tired. I was in the middle of nowhere, with Jasper still 50 miles away. I sat down on a stump beside the road and said a prayer. I admitted that I was stupid to be hitchhiking so far, or at all.

After inspecting the blisters on my heels and changing my socks, I erected my tired frame. Feeling weary, I raised my arm once more in supplication and hoped my thumb would draw attention to this despairing old man. Sure enough the heavens had mercy on me. Someone stopped and took me all the way to Hinton, about 45 miles past Jasper. I bought the man breakfast. Then, refreshed in body and spirit, I was ready to try out my good fortune again to reach Edmonton.

I was hardly out of town when a car stopped and the driver, a physician, invited me to take a seat in the back. He had one other passenger in the front seat with him. The doctor was in conversation with the other passenger, which did not interest me. I mentioned my sore feet and my fatigue and excused myself to fall asleep. That was fine with them, and I managed to sleep for a while.

When we came closer to Edmonton, I asked if he could drop me off at the West Edmonton Mall, saying that 'my better half' could pick me up from there. He, in turn, asked where I lived and said he would take me home because of my sore feet. I politely refused, embarrassed at the thought that he would see my comfortable home in an upscale neighbourhood and wonder why this guy was hitchhiking when he could easily afford a bus ticket, if not a train.

And so, with determination, I made it home. I guess I proved the saying, "There's not a man with more endurance than the man that sells insurance."

34

DEFLATED EGO
(what does it take
to run a marathon?)

Bar Harbor, Michigan

I had run several marathons in the past. This one was one of the toughest and most exhausting to date. It's your legs, you understand, that do most of the work.

The upper part of the body has the oxygen tank and the blood bank from which arteries carry oxygen-rich red blood cells to the screaming body parts, feeding the muscles with fresh air. The blood vessels also carry glucose, the stored energy that feeds the engine of movement, and that energy supply can be depleted quite rapidly. In order to store glucose, the body has to adjust to heavy use of this vital substance. That's where the training comes in. The body needs to adapt and be able to store large amounts of that sugar type to sustain vigour, or stamina if you will.

Diet is also important. A few days before the run, a runner must take in mostly proteins; then, the last few days, mostly carbohydrates. This is partly to keep the bowels happy for smooth excretion. Sometimes a runner has to make a pit stop, occasionally not making it to one of the outhouses strategically positioned at various locations throughout the run.

Bar Harbor is situated just across the Lake Huron inlet from Sarnia, Ontario. I had been invited to attend a meeting in Toronto and decided to make a side trip the week before to join some 100 or more macho speed freaks to run the 42-kilometer foot race. (This is the Canadian equivalent of the USA's 26 miles-and-a-few-hundred-yards marathon.)

I took a flight to Toronto on Friday morning and planned to change planes at Pearson Airport for the short flight to Sarnia. However, the flight was cancelled and, although I was offered a later flight, it was too much later. Instead I accepted the offer to be transported by bus. I arrived in Sarnia at about 6 p.m., took a taxi across the border and booked into a motel not far from the starting point of the race.

For supper I washed down a light meal with a glass of Coors Light beer. The next morning I got up at 6 a.m. in order to be on time for the 7 a.m. start. After my usual pancakes with syrup, followed by bathroom trips to prevent possible embarrassment, I proceeded to do a warm up of 5 to 10 minutes' jogging.

Then I was set to go to the starting point. A little nervous, I took my last swallow of water. (I have lost as much as 3 litres of fluid on a long run.) Water stations were placed every 5 miles, officials were spaced out over the length of the race, and stopwatches were set. Off we went! Right on time.

I was conditioned to run 10 miles without taking in fluids, so I normally did not drink any water at the first stop. This time, though, I knew it would be important to take in some fluids right from the beginning. Indeed, the temperature was 60°F at the start and steadily rose to 80°F by 11 a.m. (Actually, all runners are in a hurry and are quick about downing the water handed to them at each water station. More often than not, they drink only part of it and throw the rest over their heads to cool themselves off.)

We ran out of town through a tree-lined suburban area, onto a slightly undulating rural road. I was moving briskly—a seven-minute mile pace—but soon realized I would not be able to keep it up in the increasing heat. There were no refreshing breezes stirring.

By the halfway point, I was about in the middle of the whole pack of runners. I kept glancing around to see where others in my senior age category were in relation to me. Going into my third hour my legs began to cramp and I had to massage them. After that I stopped every 5 miles, then every 3 miles, but was determined not to give up. This resulted in some runners passing me. It bugged me that a spindly senior runner was getting ahead of me.

I managed to reach the end point in 3 hours and 43 minutes, averaging roughly 8.5 minutes per mile. I was exhausted and weak. Still, I was ahead of quite a few runners. I waited until everyone checked in and was rewarded with a bottle of orange juice for being third in my category of senior runners.

It had been a cruel run! I stumbled more than walked to my motel. I drank some water before reaching the motel then started on the orange juice. Orange juice contains a lot of acid and caused me to vomit bile while taking a shower.

What a miserable end to a race—a race that, in the past, I usually ended by joining some comrades in hoisting a beer or two. When a fellow runner offered me a ride to Lansing, we figured we'd stop, before leaving Port Huron, to get some of that beer after all, along with some food, to reconstitute our energy. This time it didn't work.

It wasn't until we reached Lansing that I began to feel better. Eating a banana split with a good squirt of crème de cacao really did the trick; I could feel a stream of some revival substance going in to restore my equilibrium.

Feeling more in tune with myself, I continued on from Lansing by bus to visit a cousin in Grand Rapids. From Grand Rapids, it was back to Toronto for a few days to attend the meeting, and then finally back to Edmonton.

At home again, having dinner with my family (our three daughters still lived at home) I was questioned about my recent trip to Toronto and the side excursion to Port Huron. Despite my trials in running the marathon and my disappointment, I made the best of my story. I had come in ahead of others in my age class, and I proudly showed my souvenir of coming in third. Then Marianne, my youngest daughter, who was then 16, piped up and asked, "How many senior runners were in your category, Dad? Three? Two months later I ran another marathon in Seattle, WA—45° and drizzling, time: 3.13.

35

MOTOR HOME TRAVEL, PART I

Finally we had the finances in place to buy a home on wheels. We had been looking in various places to find a vehicle that would suit our purpose of traveling in style to an RV resort in Apache Junction, Arizona.

To get acquainted with this type of a behemoth, we had rented one, two years earlier, for a weekend to Jasper National Park. We wanted to get the feel of driving and manoeuvring such a large vehicle in and around campgrounds and to feel comfortable driving it on highways. It was also important to get to know the mechanical requirements of a day in a motor home.

Wanting to leave on New Year's Day, we picked up our "Bessie", as we named her, from the dealership on New Year's Eve. It was about 20° below zero when the salesmen drove the vehicle out of its warm showroom onto the parking lot for us to drive home. Wanting to be ready for departure the following afternoon we loaded some of our food and clothing into our newly acquired home on wheels. I also connected an electrical extension cord to what I thought was the engine block heater. We were happy and full of anticipation about being on our way the next day.

The next morning, being conscientious church-goers, we attended the New Year's Day service, and then quickly went home to get a bite to eat and head out for the South.

The temperature that morning was -25°. While my wife, Grace, got the last items together for loading, I went to start the engine for a warm up. It would not start. The engine would hardly turn over and did not fire. I wondered what could be wrong. Exiting the motor home, I checked the electric cable I had attached to the block heater the day before and found it to be incorrectly connected. Correcting the problem would not suddenly warm up the engine; it would take some time. By this time, the battery was nearly dead, and we had no battery charger. I decided to disconnect the car, which was already hooked up to the rear of the motor home, and park it near enough to use jumper cables and recharge the batteries on the motor home.

In the meantime, my friendly neighbour saw me struggling and came to my rescue, bringing and hooking up his battery charger. After waiting half an hour, I tried to start the engine again. No luck; the engine only fired once, belting out a little smoke from the exhaust pipe. It was still too stiff and the battery was still not sufficiently charged. We left the car running, to do the charging, while Grace and I went inside for a cup of coffee to discuss the situation, almost giving up on leaving that day.

An hour later we decided to give it one more try. By this time, lo and behold, the heating element had done its work. The engine burped, then fired again, sputtered some more, and then took hold, belching thick clouds of smoke, and finally running smoothly. Thank heavens, it was only 3 p.m. and there was still time to drive it for a few hours before darkness set in.

Off we went, steering Bessie south on the highway. In the meantime, I did not feel well; with all the frustrations and the cold weather I'd worked in, I felt feverish. Grace, in turn, felt exhausted from loading and then unloading when it looked like we might not get on our way.

After a few hours' drive we stopped at a roadside restaurant for something to eat. We ordered a light supper, which tasted soggy; old turkey leftover from Christmas servings no doubt. Before leaving again I took a few tablets of Tylenol to get rid of the cold shivers I was experiencing. They worked, calming my body, and I felt much better after that.

In the meantime, we passed Calgary. The sky was clearing, bright stars were twinkling in the heavens, and the roads were smooth. Things were looking up as we headed for Lethbridge.

In Lethbridge, we stopped at a major Esso service station to top up the fuel thank and then asked permission to park behind the station overnight. The attendants hesitated at first, but, with some persuasion, they even let us hook up to their electric power outlet. Then we enjoyed a restful night. The temperature was only -5°F.

Next morning, January 2nd, we had an early start. I remembered to disconnect the electric power line from our host, and checked the hitching bar on our towed car. We drove for an hour and stopped for breakfast in a small village before crossing the U.S. border. The road was clear of snow, and we were moving along nicely, gradually gaining altitude.

We were approaching the mountains. As we reached the Monida pass, at an altitude of nearly 7000 feet, driving was suddenly no longer relaxed. The roadbed became rough, requiring close attention. It had snowed the day before and partly melted, forming a rough surface. The dishes and other loose things in the cupboards rattled behind us. It was a long, lonely, rough stretch of highway. Driving at a reduced speed we reached Idaho Falls about 5 p.m. Being unfamiliar with this area, I asked a service station attendant for a good place to stay overnight. He suggested carrying on for another 5 miles to a truck stop where I would find adequate room, so we moved on. I checked the odometer, not to miss the exit, but did anyway. Grace was not pleased, to say the least. Visibility was much reduced as darkness descended on us. She was worried about where we would find a spot to park overnight. She wanted me to turn around, but I managed to calm her down, explaining that the next town was only 45 miles ahead. I reassured her that we could find a nice spot, there, to stay overnight.

We reached Pocatello, Idaho, about 7 p.m. Turning off at the first exit, we saw a large shopping center and parked ourselves on the edge of the parking lot, out of the way of smaller vehicles. We let out a big sigh of relief, happy that all was well so far. Taking notice of a restaurant, we treated ourselves to a piece of pie and coffee. Later, back inside our home on wheels, we watched TV for a while and then retired early.

Next morning, we were awakened early by a snowplough. It shocked me at first, but it was nothing to worry about; there was only one inch of snow on the ground.

Continuing on our journey, we traveled at a lower altitude—no mountain passes to worry about. The highway was ploughed, free of snow, and we moved at a moderate pace. Passing Salt Lake City, Grace took note of the fuel gauge and thought it might be getting close to empty and asked if I would please find a service station pronto. I protested, but she insisted. I swerved off at the next exit that indicated a small town. To my consternation, the roads were treacherous. There had been a heavy snowfall the night before, and, while the highway had been ploughed clean, the side roads had not.

Spying a service station on a somewhat narrow street, we approached it cautiously. I saw that it was too small for a big motor home to enter and, furthermore, it did not sell diesel fuel. There was no chance to turn around, so I choose to drive on through a residential area and was worried that we might get stuck in a dead end. Some coarse language passed my lips. Fortunately, we were able to manoeuvre our way around the block and reached the highway again. Relieved, I did what I should have done before; I called on my trucking friends for advice on where to obtain diesel fuel. We probably had enough fuel yet for a while, but it is better to be safe than sorry; to have a full tank of fuel instead of being stranded in the middle of nowhere. Not too many miles down the road was a spacious truck stop where we filled our fuel tank.

Our next objective was to reach St. George, Utah, a distance of about 450 miles from our last overnight stay in Pocatello. We had to go over one more pass at a height of 5800 feet. Thankfully, it was clear and we arrived in St. George about 5 p.m. I knew were the RV Park was located, having seen it two years earlier when we passed through this place by car. (It was also the place where I had been hospitalized for nearly a week a few years before, but that is another story.)

After we registered our rig and car and settled into this RV Park, our friends Gurben and Alice Hulzenga showed up with their 5th Wheel. They had left Edmonton very early the morning after we left, hoping to catch up with us, and there they were, surprised and happy to meet us there. We had a nice get-together that evening, sharing supper and playing canasta, our favourite card game.

The following morning, somewhat anxious about getting to our final destination, we were ready to leave right after breakfast. We had made sure all was ready with our motor home, especially the connections to our car that we pulled behind us. Everything seemed in order. We started Bessie and slowly crawled out of our parking lot onto the road leading to the main road. All of a sudden, I heard someone yelling. I stopped and noticed that, as I took my foot off the accelerator, the motor home stopped instantly. I quickly got out from behind the steering wheel and went outside, where our friends told me that I had forgotten to release the brakes on the car we were pulling. Mad at myself for this oversight, I started Bessie up again and continued.

We had traveled some distance when I heard a strange noise that appeared to come from the roof. Again I stopped, and checked to see what might be the problem this time. I had forgotten to crank down the TV antenna from within the motor home. Another lesson learned, I wondered what else there was for me to discover or what I had not been cautious enough about. What I did learn is to make a list of all the things I should check before departure, just like an aircraft pilot checks his large console, the flashing lights revealing his readiness status. I felt a bit ashamed and derided myself again for inattention to detail.

We traveled on toward Las Vegas, where we planned to make another fuel stop and wash down our motor home and car; both were terribly dirty from melted snow, sand, and salt on the road. After our sandwich stop in Las Vegas, in mild weather, our mobile home was clean as a whistle. All ship shape, we moved on. We had only 300 miles left to go, five to six more hours to Apache Junction, AZ.

Because it was getting dark, we thought of making an overnight stop in Wickenburg. But after stopping for coffee and a snack, we decided to motor on because we knew the route, and we wanted to avoid the morning rush hour in Phoenix.

We arrived at about 10 pm and pulled into "our" Roadhaven RV resort, parking our rig on the lot that we had bought the year before. We were tired and ready to go to bed, but first we drank a glass of wine to toast and celebrate our safe arrival. We wintered there until April of that year (1993).

36

MOTOR HOME TRAVEL, PART II

Our first experience in driving our newly-acquired motor home was through snow and cold weather to Arizona was during the winter of 1992-93. This story takes us from there to our next trips.

We felt comfortable living in the motor home for more than three months, from January through April. We remained stationary in our RV resort in Apache Junction, Arizona. Our resort had many amenities, such as a swimming pool, a golf course, a poolroom, tennis courts, hobby shops and a computer room. There was no reason to be bored.

Grace liked the idea of staying put in an established community, instead of changing places and roaming around the country. We owned our spot in this RV resort and improved it with a cement driveway and a spacious patio. We built a shed, which included a washer, a dryer, a sink, and a water heater, besides room to store our patio set while absent.

Planning a trip is often more fun than the actual experience, we found out. We took our motor home out of storage on the first of October and prepared it for departure the following day. This meant loading it with food and clothing and filling the tanks with fuel and water. To our annoyance, we found an inch of snow on the ground the following morning. The forecast was for warmer weather, however, so we felt comfortable leaving anyway.

Surprise, surprise. The snow we had in Alberta moved east into Saskatchewan and came down in greater amounts. As the day progressed and we got closer to Regina, there was snow on the side of the roads and the pavement was a bit slushy. We decided to find a place to camp and saw a sign for camping at Lumsden. Turning off, we found that the campground was deep in snow and not suitable for a motor home. Fortunately, there was a spacious service station next to it and we received permission to stay overnight.

Being self-sufficient, with a generator for power, lights and TV and a propane gas for cooking, we made and ate supper, then watched a movie. We shut down our noisy generator at 10 p.m., set the thermostat to 65°F (18° C), crawled under our cozy down blanket, and went off to Dreamland.

We were awakened at 5 a.m. by a strange sound. There was no time for yawning as I realized that the utility batteries where drained. With the temperature having dropped to -10F, the heater was using more juice than expected. Quick action was required. Should I unhook the car to recharge the batteries using the jumper cables? What about the main engine, would it start? I thought it was worth a try, and thank heavens it started. What a relief! With the main engine running, the utility battery automatically re-charges. Unfortunately, the water line was frozen, so we skipped breakfast.

Getting on our way again in semi darkness, we passed Regina on the ring road, heading for the U.S. border. The sun was rising, warming the day to above freezing. We stopped in a small town for fuel and had a hearty breakfast of bacon and eggs in at the adjacent café. In the meantime, the water line had thawed out. Things were looking up! With renewed anticipation, we looked forward to what the day would bring.

We spent a few days in Rapid City doing some sightseeing. There we came across some free-ranging donkeys in a nearby park. One felt free to stick his face into our open driver's side window looking for a hand out. I was not in the mood to have him almost nibbling at my ears. I moved the car slowly ahead so he would withdraw his wet nose from my face; I had nothing to offer him.

We moved on to our next objective, to visit the sculptured profiles of three past presidents, carved out of a mountainside. Very impressive! It had taken about two decades to complete this dangerous work, since it was interrupted for a number of years due to economic depression.

Motoring on the next day, going southwest, we connected with Interstate 25. We bypassed Denver on the ring road at an elevation of about 5000 feet. The weather was balmy and we made good time.

We reached Santa Fe, New Mexico, in mid-afternoon, a most delightful place with Pueblo-type architecture. In the 16th century, the Spanish conquistadors entered this territory. They created a vibrant culture with the native Indians and left a rich history. We spent two days exploring. While enjoying the interesting architecture of the town, we visited a clothing store. The fashionable, colourful and feminine dresses overwhelmed my senses to the point of hurting my eyeballs. I was almost ready to buy one for Grace, but the price was too high. Besides, Grace would not want to wear such an extravagance. Still, I felt heady, visualizing Grace in such a fabulously attractive dress. We left Santa Fe and our yet-to-explore surroundings. The place left an indelible impression on us; we promised to return to the area in the future.

We had intended to fuel up before leaving Santa Fe, but we missed the exit for the service station. Well, I reckoned, we should have more than enough to reach Albuquerque. Grace objected but I paid no heed, explaining that Albuquerque was only 50 miles away and, according to the information about our motor home, we should have enough fuel for another 100 miles. I ignored the fuel gauge, which indicated that we were low.

Nearing Albuquerque, we slowed down then stopped along the side of the road to view a spectacle in the sky above us: dozens of colourful hot air balloons. It was the annual balloon festival, with balloonists coming together from all over the country. The balloons came in all different shapes, sizes and designs, in the form of animals and other recognizable objects.

Moving on towards Albuquerque on a three-lane highway, rubber posts funnelled us into a single lane on the left. The other lanes were being repaved. Suddenly, our big engine sputtered, then quit. I just had enough speed to move between the barricades and into the middle lane, ending up under a bridge. After this whirlwind action, I was in traumatic state of mind, sweating. A paving crew was getting ready to pave the two lanes beside us. What should I do? I panicked. I had to get out of their way!

Then I thought of the "Citizen Band Radio" (CB); I could call for help. I grabbed the handheld speaker and shouted, "Mayday, mayday!" I didn't know what else to say; I didn't even know our whereabouts in the city. No one answered my cry over the airwaves. It was Sunday morning; there were no truckers on the road.

Then Grace reminded me we had a car we could unhook and use to get fuel. Thus, this sweet woman calmed my excited state of mind. We removed the car from its umbilical cord and proceeded to look for a service station. Still in a state of angst and not wanting to lose my way in finding a service station, I drove up a down ramp. A few horns blasted, but I paid no attention. I made a right-hand turn onto the overpass below which our motor home was parked. Only a block away was a service station where we could get some diesel fuel. However, since we did not have a container, we had to go a few more blocks to a store to buy one. Then it was back to the station to fill it and then return to our motor home.

After pouring the diesel into the fuel tank, I got behind the wheel and turned the starting button. Nothing happened. I tried again, but, no sir, it would not start. I was getting red in the face and wondered what was wrong with the blasted vehicle, when a paving crewmember came to tell me to get out of the way; they had to pave this stretch of road. "I would be glad to move this S.O.B. out the way but I can't get it started," I countered. "I need a mechanic."

"OK we'll send you one," and he got on his walkie-talkie and called their mechanic to come over. I explained to him what had happened, and he told me to prime the fuel pump. I asked him to please show me how this is done and he did. After all, he had to get rid of us. I got back into this bugger on wheels, and cranked the engine. This time, it started easily and the engine ran as if nothing had happened.

Thanking the Good Samaritan, I sat behind the steering wheel, as Grace was getting into her seat, and took a deep breath, trying to relax. As I put the behemoth into gear and slowly started moving towards the barricades to get back in the left lane, I looked into my rearview mirror and saw that we had left our little towing car behind. With all the hoopla, we forgot to attach it to its mother again. With another sigh of exasperation, we hooked up the car. Off we went, not speaking to one another. Even after filling the tank with fuel at a truck stop, it took a few miles until our accosted brains relaxed and our breathing became more normal.

We had only two days of travel left to reach our winter resting place in Apache Junction. We yearned for our permanent spot in the Road Haven RV resort. Once we were parked and hooked up to water and electricity there, we could enjoy the winter in peace without motor home worries.

Meanwhile, we spent the night in an RV park. The next morning, we followed Interstate 40 West. I consulted the map for directions, and decided to turn off at Holbrook, towards Mesa, AZ, via Payson. Still traveling south, I missed the cut-off, but thought, Oh, well, the road is quite nice and not winding much. This was so until we reached the Salt Lake Canyon. From there on, the road wound down steeply through the mountains. Driving a large and heavy motor home with a car behind us, pushing us down the winding canyon roads, is not my favourite activity. Even though the canyon road was very scenic, I have little recollection of that scenery, being terribly busy steering and watching traffic in front and behind. To gear down on steep slopes, one always has to be prepared to do so before you are in the downward stretch. Needless to say, it was not a relaxing end to our drive; it was hair-raising.

Some years later I deceived myself into, or succumbed to the allure of, buying a new motor home. Oh, it seemed like heaven on wheels—so colourful, more spacious, a more powerful motor and so many amenities, not to mention the big discount—too good to pass up. It was a beauty all right. My friends and neighbours admired it, too; so nice and shiny.

After driving it for a year it gave us pause to reconsider, however. One of the first problems we encountered was the windshield wipers breaking down during a rainstorm. We were laid up an entire day, waiting for new parts to arrive. Next, we found out that the batteries would not hold their electric charge very long. This motor home, before we bought it, had been sitting on the sales lot for over a year, causing the batteries to deteriorate. They needed replacement.

Then there was a big motor home convention in Las Cruces, New Mexico. We had to go! There were a thousand new motor homes for viewing and sale. Along with some friends who were also very enthusiastic RVers we admired them alright. But after a few days, we got to wondering and asked ourselves, What is so important? What do we gain by admiring newer and bigger motor homes that we can't afford? Is consumerism getting to us?

Grace already had the answer, and was in favour of quitting this motor home business. I was less convinced, until two incidents occurred to change my mind.

Firstly, on our return from the convention we ran into a sand storm, which threatened to blow us off the road. We needed a place to stay until the storm abated. Secondly, we needed to dump our sewage somewhere. We found a place to dump, but could not park our rig close enough for convenience. We had to stretch out our sewer hose to its limit, and then, when I twisted the handle for the tank to drain, the force of the stinky excrement caused the hose to slip out of the drain hole, making a terrible mess around the area. Grace, already upset with the weather and cold temperature, let out a scream in desperation. She worried that the feces might contaminate us somehow.

That evening we camped in a very peaceful campground and had time to vent our frustrations. Grace was now more than ready to give up on our motor home. I wasn't quite there, but was now open for discussion.

Arriving at our usual R.V. resort the next day, we went back to our normal routine. For me it was going for a daily swim, spending time in the computer club and reading. For Grace, it was picking up her pencil to draw or her paint brush for water colour painting.

For several days I debated with myself, whether or not to sell this motor home. I could buy a mobile home in its place, which would become our permanent place to stay during winter months. While swimming, I had time to think and reason with myself. Praying for guidance, I came to the conclusion that I had been seduced by the idea that bigger is better and by frills. Grace had the right idea: let's sell it.

Decision made, we sold our motor home soon after arriving home from Arizona, without much depreciation from our acquisition price. We have no regrets!

37

RUSSIA
(and its black market)

My university studies ended in 1987 with a course in Russian history. As part of the course, I read a book written by a journalist who had lived in Russia for a number of years. This journalist left Russia in 1985 and pointed out the inconsistency between what-the-Republic-of-Russia-wanted-us-to-believe about life in Russia and the experience of the people; the average person on the street understood the difference between official statements and reality.

With this on my mind, I had the urge to visit Russia and explore for myself what the country was like in the past and in the present. This was two years before the destruction of the Berlin wall, and Gorbachev was president. He had written a book called <u>Perestroika</u>, meaning "openness".

In order to travel to Russia one must go via Europe. This gave me an opportunity to visit my brothers in Holland. Thinking to encourage one or two of them to come along with me on my journey, I contacted them in advance with the proposal. Within a week, I received word that all of my four brothers would join me, and I arranged for all of us to join a tour group going to St. Petersburg and Moscow.

I was very happy that my brothers decided to make this journey in solidarity with me. I bought five corduroy baseball caps and had them embroidered with our first names and our family logo—the name "Ruiter" with a horse and rider. My brothers are all tall, six feet or more, and, whenever we mingled with our other tour group members on excursions, we could spot the hats from afar.

Our first stop was Leningrad, now St. Petersburg. Walking down a shopping street without our Russian guide, a man approached me and asked if I would exchange American dollars for Russian rubles. He offered me fifty rubles for twenty American dollars. I had just bought rubles at a fixed exchange rate of one ruble for three dollars, so I thought this is a good deal. He led me to a shop, out of sight of prying eyes, and we made the exchange. The bank notes marked "fifty", which I assumed were rubles, turned out to be worthless Yugoslavian currency. I had been swindled by a con artist and he was gone like the wind.

That was my first lesson in the black market. Even though I had actually done some research on it, I found I needed more experience before getting involved again. Others in our group were unhappy with my actions, fearing we would all get into trouble.

The next day our guide and interpreter, who spoke fairly good Dutch, escorted us to the various museums. We had a modern bus and a chauffer at our disposal. The bus was comfortable; the local buses were wrecks in comparison. The buildings in St. Petersburg were in disrepair and in desperate need of paint. In the evening, without our guide, some of us explored the city by foot with the assistance of one fellow tourist who spoke reasonable Russian. We tried out the underground rail system, which ran frequently and was comfortable. That was one thing the Russians could be proud about, and a ride was only a nickel per person.

After three days sightseeing in St. Petersburg we left for Moscow on an Aeroflot flight. We stayed in a four-star hotel, where the food was plentiful and fairly good. Certainly it was more than the local people had and of better quality. There was also a confectionery, where you could by souvenirs and liquors. It accepted foreign currency only.

Again, in Moscow, the Dutch-speaking guide took us to the famous sites. We visited Red Square and the Kremlin buildings where one could stand in line to view Lenin's mausoleum. I was not interested in standing in line to see the dead body of Lenin, so, along with a few others, I went to the shopping mall, the pride of Moscow (which I believe was called "G.U.M", meaning Great Universal Mall). It was nothing in comparison to our malls in Canada, or Europe for that matter. I enjoyed just watching people and took notice of a few young people exchanging money. The clothing people wore was colourless and drab. In fact, one young fellow asked if he could buy my light blue jacket right off my back. That was a "No"; I needed to stay warm myself.

When I did decide to buy a few trinkets to take home, I discovered I was short of rubles. That reminded me of the young fellows I had seen exchanging money. In spite of my disastrous previous incident, I was determined not to exchange my dollars at the paltry official rate. I looked for those fellows I had seen earlier and asked them if they were interested in some cigarettes. They gave me three rubles per pack of Pall mal cigarettes! With this windfall, I made up for my earlier loss and was able to make my purchases.

Now that I had better knowledge of the local currency and some experience, I decided to make another trade. Before leaving Canada I had purchased a pair of jeans that would fit a young person. I wanted to use these to practice my skill in trading. I made contact with a black marketer at an underground train exit. He was interested in my merchandise and we agreed to meet at the hotel's spiral stairway, out of sight of the security guard at the entrance. I thought I would be safe there; in case of trouble I could shout or take flight up the stairs into the hotel. The jeans cost $20.00, the equivalent of almost seven Russian rubles, and I sold them for ninety rubles, the equivalent of $270.00 Canadian dollars. Then, just as I pocketed the money and the other fellow stuffed the jeans under his coat, a security guard came bouncing down the steps. My young trader took off and I looked dumbly at the guard. He turned his pocket inside out to ask me if I was being hustled by a pickpocket. Shakily, I nodded and scurried back to my hotel room.

Once I recovered, I wondered what to do with ninety rubles? I couldn't spend it in the confectionery of the establishment where we were staying. It would be a shame to be stuck with them. I would not be able to go back to the official exchange office, since I could not prove I bought them there. Fortunately, on my way to dinner that evening in the hotel lobby, I saw some bottles of wine for sale, priced in rubles. I bought four bottles, which I shared with my travel companions. This wine originated in the country of Georgia, and we toasted our Russian experience.

On our last evening in Moscow we attended an opera in the world-famous Bolshoi Theatre. It was expensive, but that was the Russian way of milking tourists of their foreign currency. We were seated in a box on the third floor where, in earlier days, the Russian royalties had sat. They played a Tchaikovsky piece. The acoustics were great, the music intoxicating. My face was flushed with excitement, and I felt higher than a kite. My brothers were equally impressed, and at the end of the performance we shouted, "Bravo! Bravo!" Unfortunately, our neighbours in the same box were not so enthralled with our boisterous applause. The following day we traveled back to Holland where we were welcomed at the airport by our wives and a sister. As always, it was good to be home, telling our stories.

38

RUSSIA AND CULTURE

I graduated from The King's University College, in Edmonton, AB, in May 1987 with a major in history. History was my favourite subject, firstly because it evoked images of adventure and made me aware of mankind's foibles. Secondly, I was interested in the church and its spiritual impact in times and places of the past

I think that we in the twentieth century can be very condescending about events in the past when we do not consider the historical time frame or context, including the prevailing perceptions of truth and knowledge.

Having finished a study of Russian history in our last semester in college, I took a special interest in the Russian Orthodox Church. I was fascinated by the way in which God used His human creatures to make His presence known throughout the world. The following story is about how I was struck, in unexpected places, with revelation concerning how God's Spirit flows.

In 988 AD Russian Prince Vladimir, from Kiev, traveled down the Dnepr River and crossed the Black Sea to Constantinople, now called Istanbul, in Turkey. (The total distance was about 1000 kilometres.) Prince Vladimir was on a trading mission and came into contact with the Greek Orthodox Church. (This church had separated from the Roman Catholic Church in the 10th century over a theological dispute.) When Prince Vladimir visited a certain cathedral, its splendour mesmerized him. The majestic rituals, as well as the mosaics, the frescoes and other beautiful decorations, exuded power and so intoxicated the prince that he adopted the Greek Orthodox religion as his own. He also found his bride there, which added to his admiration of the church.

Returning to Kiev from Constantinople, the Prince became a missionary for change. He turned his people from the pagan practices of idol worship to the redeeming Word of God and to the worship of God, Christ and the Holy Spirit. Thus the Russian Orthodox Church had its beginning in 988 AD. It is still the dominant church group in Russia today.

I traveled to Russia that year, 1987, when Gorbachev was in power in the U. S. S. R. It was two years before the Berlin wall was torn down.

Arriving in Moscow by air with other tourists, we were welcomed with first-class accommodations, including five-star hotels and modern buses. We had no opportunity to see the flats or houses in which the local people lived, but we saw that the local buses were shabby and poorly maintained. Tourists were usually guided to places where buildings were in good repair. They were shown museums and a few cathedrals to impress them and make them believe that all was well under communist rule.

We visited some of those churches. One had a service in progress. This aroused my interest, and I watched the goings on. Unfortunately, most people in attendance at the service were standing, which meant that I could see very little of the priest and his movements. I could hear the a cappella singing, however, which I found very beautiful. Although my mind was still in a prejudiced mode and I had mixed feelings about their overall style of worship, my interest in the Russian Orthodox Church remained strong; it needed more exploration.

Opportunity presented itself. There was a bus going to Zagorsk, some 50 miles from the hotel or an hour's distance from Moscow. Zagorsk is where the Russian Orthodox Church has its seminary and several churches.

First, the guide led us to a museum of history where much jewellery and many ornaments and vestments were displayed. It did not take long before I got bored listening to the guide and made my escape to a nearby church where a service was in progress.

Fortunately, it was not busy; I had a clear view of the ceremony and watched it all. I still had a prejudicial view of the Russian Orthodox Church, feeling that there were many remnants of paganism, i.e. icons, elaborate vestments, the miter and the staff—with its icon of Jesus on the crossbeam—which worshippers may kiss.

As the procession of priests passed by, dressed in their splendid vestments and carrying their staffs, I heard a chorus of a cappella singing. Suddenly, I felt vibrations running through me and heard a voice in my head saying, "Francis, who are you to judge where and how God's Spirit flows?" I felt stricken, shaken in my boots. I sat down trying to unravel my thoughts. I decided to let go of my intellectual reasoning, with my Protestant-coloured glasses and my assumption that I knew how God's Spirit works.

How God's Spirit works is a mystery!

Later, I read an article which gave me some explanation. It said, "Words, sounds and pictures are equally valued and are valid means of communication in glorifying the faith." This experience made a deep impression on my spiritual life. The following song lyrics come to my mind: "I know not how the Spirit moves convincing men of sin."

With this experience behind me, I attended an ecclesiastic assembly in 1988 where syncretism (the attempted blending of irreconcilable principles was discussed.) The above story came to my mind, and I formed the following conclusion:

We in the Christian Reformed church are in involved with native people in Canada. We wish to share with them the Gospel of Jesus Christ and how it relates to our daily lives and our treatment of our neighbours. To share the Gospel with our native brethren, we have to understand their culture and their spiritual past. Together, we need to comprehend each other's cultures as a springboard for showing them how Christ's redemption works in us and can enrich our lives and give us comfort. We want to show them that God will take care of all cultures and people who follow His precepts. In short, we need to love God above all and our fellow man as ourselves. (From Mathew 22:4-40) I believe the controversy about symbols falls away and becomes irrelevant when one can place them in historic context.

We have a native healing centre in Edmonton. Because I wanted some experience with symbols, I invited myself to attend a prayer circle which uses a sweat lodge and the sweet-grass smudge. The native elder in charge of the prayer circle welcomed me into their midst and I was invited to participate in the prayer, which I did. It was a good experience and a chance to testify about my faith life.

The natives' use of the sweat lodge is two-fold: for cleansing the body and, symbolically, for purification of the soul. The sweet-grass smudge is similar to the incense used in the Catholic and Anglican churches, with which we share church creeds. It is not an impediment to reaching out and embracing the Christian faith.

When we are Spirit-led, all props, statues or mementos fall away. Therefore, there are no irreconcilable differences between the (white) Christian faith and our native Canadians who want to accept the Christian faith. Let us not use the Bible as a textbook of how to worship, but as an aid to God's promises of redemption. Sometimes we forget who God is when we cram Him into doctrinal boxes and squabble over this and that!

39

GOD'S SUSTAINING HANDS THROUGH TRIAL AND PAIN

"The boundary lines have fallen for me in pleasant places;
surely I have a delightful inheritance."
(Psalm 16:6, NIV)

Arriving on bicycle in Neerlandia, after traveling a distance of some 100 miles, my grandson, Levi, age 6, asked me: "Grand-dad, did you cycle all the way from Edmonton?"

"Yes," I said.

Levi then looked up at me again and said, "But you are old!"

I was fifty-eight at the time.

It was a beautiful day the following Monday in August, 1987. I worked in the garden that morning for a while, picking beans for canning. After preparing the beans for cooking I left to go for an hour bicycle ride, planning to be back at lunchtime. I love to be active outdoors, and, since just a few days before I had completed this long bike ride, I figured I'd enjoy a short ride.

At lunch time, I did not show up as Grace had expected. Instead, the doorbell sounded and, when she opened the door, there was a police officer facing her. He asked if she was Mrs. Ruiter. She smiled and said yes, having no notion of the news she was facing. The policeman explained that her husband was in the hospital as a result of a bicycle accident, and asked if he could accompany her to the hospital. Grace hesitated, somewhat bewildered, saying she wasn't dressed for that and was in the middle of canning. He suggested she should come as she was, entered the kitchen with her to make sure the stove was turned off, then drove her to the hospital. En route he asked her about our children and how he could reach them. He did not tell her that her husband had arrived at the hospital near death because of serious blood loss.

At the hospital, Grace was met by the chaplain who took her to my bedside in the emergency ward. There she was informed of what state I was in, and that it might be necessary to amputate my left leg. Again, Grace felt bewildered and could not quite comprehend what had happened, or how serious the multiple injuries were.

In the meantime, the officer who had brought Grace to the hospital went to pick up our daughter Marianne from her job at the grocery store, Safeway. Linda, our other daughter who was attending her own child at the Royal Alex Hospital, was informed by telephone of her dad's accident and asked to come. She hurried to where I was, at the Misericordia Hospital. The chaplain called our minister, Pastor DeWaal, and he came to comfort the family, since my condition was considered very serious.

All of this I have gathered from the recollections of family and visitors. Personally, I don't remember anything about the accident and that day's goings on. That evening I awoke from sedation and found Carolyn, our third daughter, and her husband, Phil, standing by my bedside. They looked concerned, but said nothing. So I started the conversation by asking them if they had seen the new rattan furniture we bought. They could not grasp this question, thinking I must be delirious given the bad shape I was in. Maybe I was.

It took several days before I began to understand what had happened and what the prospects of healing were. The machinery on my bedside with wires leading into my nostrils and mouth and needles sticking in my veins, the wide collar around my neck, and the needles stuck periodically into my buttocks did not give me a clear picture of the situation. Asking questions over the next few days, I became aware of some of the particulars of what happened. While riding my bicycle, I had been hit from behind by a motor vehicle and left in the ditch on a rural road. A retired nurse and her husband had witnessed the accident from a distance and the nurse had made a tourniquet to restrict the bleeding. Another passerby with a cellular phone called 911 for an ambulance.

I was saved from death. I believed this to be God's intervention to save me for the sake of my family and possibly for use by His grace. I remember while cycling one day some months earlier on the shoulder of Highway 16, thinking about the possibility of being struck by a motor vehicle. I thought to myself, Yes, it could happen. Just because you pray for safety, you are not automatically excluded from mishaps! Therefore cycle on!

I did not know the painful road ahead of me, of being hospitalized for a total of about five months, off and on, over a period of nearly three years, and being on crutches as well. I was in the operating room about eight times for bone grafts (three of them would not take) and, later, for revisions of the amputated stump. The first operation on my left leg involved screwing the foot back on to the ankle and having steel pins stuck into drilled holes of the tibia to keep them aligned. The most excruciating pain was after the reconstruction of the shattered leg when the bandaging was lifted from the skin-grafted wound. I could hardly bear the excruciating pain it caused.

When I took stock of my situation after the reconstruction I felt optimistic about healing. After all, this athletic fellow couldn't stay down! I was also somewhat in denial of the consequences. However, after the second bone graft six weeks later, and after enduring so much pain, the post-operation trauma brought me to tears every time someone asked me how I was doing. Three weeks before Christmas I phoned my brother in Holland from my bed at 3:00 am, when it was about noon over there, and asked him to come and visit me. He did. He and his wife Gre were over in a few days. They were good company for Grace, and helped to console both of us.

The horror that I faced after the second bone graft was that I had to be on intravenous for seven weeks. It was used to drip a toxic drug into my system to fight a persistent bone infection. The fear was that the drug could damage my kidneys and hearing. I survived with much frustration, being tied down with the drip system on a pole, always needing to find new veins to put the intravenous needles in. It taxed my patience severely!

In April 1989 the tibia would not heal, and one more time a bone graft was performed. It did not take! In January 1990 infection in the leg started up again and it became evident the leg would need to be removed. Amputation was performed on the left leg, below the knee, at the end of February 1990.

After the amputation, fitting the stump into prosthesis was not easy. The mangled condition of what was left after the operation required a number of fittings until the stump had reduced in size. A year later they did a revision for a better fit. This was repeated two years later. After numerous fittings and almost three years on crutches, I gradually improved my mobility.

It was after my amputation that I took up swimming again. I joined the new Y.M.C.A in my neighbourhood. I was and still am, very thankful for how God has sustained me through all this. I can swim to exercise my body in relative comfort and without pain. A few times someone has asked me, like Job's friends in the Bible story, if I thought God had visited me with this accident, to which I answered, "I don't believe God wants me to be handicapped, but if He did cause this accident to happen I would be honoured that he would bother with a sinner like me. Like Job, I know that my redeemer lives."

I feel blessed in many ways. I can accept my pain and my handicap, yet don't think of it much as a handicap anymore because I get around easily enough and don't miss the running and cycling. I miss the hiking somewhat, but am rewarded with time and resources to travel by other means. I have traveled to Bangladesh, Kenya and Cuba, and visiting with fellow Christians there has been a joy for me. My life is rich! There are so many ways to enjoy God's creation and I feel grateful that I still can!

40

WRESTLING MATCH IN BEIJING (2001)

My friend Peter and I had arranged to take a tour called "The Silk Route." This tour would start in Peking, China, and end up in St. Petersburg, Russia. The tour group would spend 10 days in China and then make stops in Kazakhstan and Uzbekistan. We arrived in Beijing a few days ahead of the tour guide. This gave us time to get acclimatized and to orientate ourselves before the rest of our tour group arrived.

My friend had spent some years in Hong Kong in the (nineteen) fifties and wanted to get reacquainted with that part of Asia. I was happy to join him, knowing that it would be interesting and exciting. We both had a great interest in history and this trip looked very promising in that regard.

The first day, after the buffet breakfast that was included in the price of our hotel, we did some sightseeing in the neighbourhood. We wandered around for the morning, and came across a family type restaurant for lunch a few blocks away from our lodgings. It was quite reasonable in price, and we ate using chopsticks without too much problem. A family with a young boy entered the restaurant. The father spoke English and stopped at our table to welcome us to his country. We felt honoured by this gesture and did, in fact, feel welcome.

The next day, straying a little further from our hotel, we saw a restaurant advertising Peking duck. We decided to try it out. This restaurant was classier, having tables with linen tablecloths and napkins.

I followed Peter's advice about customs and etiquette. We both ordered the dumplings and Peking duck as advertised. When our plates of Peking duck arrived, we looked somewhat aghast; the ducks were nicely arranged but their eyes were staring at us accusingly! This display certainly diminished our appetites, but we managed to twist the ducks' necks to cover their now sad eyes and ate them, albeit with less relish than we had first anticipated.

From there we strolled a few blocks further and entered a Friendship Store, so called to entice tourists to spend their money. They can be found next to every tourist attraction, and often one has to walk through the store to reach the intended object of interest.

Coming out of the store, my legs and feet were tired and getting sore. I saw a few taxis and also spied some two-wheeled chariots pulled by fairly muscular men. We approached them, and, mostly through hand signals, we were quoted 15 dollars for each vehicle. Peter was quick to get confirmation and said: "Chinese Yuan to take us to the hotel?" The man nodded his head. There was room enough for two, but the man who had to pull the rickshaw hesitated. Seeing that we were 6 ft tall and weighed two hundred pounds each, he directed us to take separate rides. We hoisted ourselves into the buggies which I later called "Chariots pulled by Spartacus."

It was rather exciting to be pulled along side streets, crossing intersections and viewing other traffic. Our chariots stopped half a block away from the hotel entrance. To be cautious, while the men pulled us along I had peeled off 15 Yuan bills from a bundle of Chinese currency and put them in a separate pocket. I did not want my Spartacus to see the amount of money I carried. When we disembarked from the rickshaws, Peter pulled his money from his pocket and gave his man 20 Yuan.

My leather-faced Spartacus saw what his cohort received and wanted the equal amount from me, which I refused because we agreed to 15 Yuan. He then grabbed me by the wrist. He was as strong as an ox. I grabbed his wrist, too, and tried to wrestle free. I didn't have a chance as he was 25 years younger and battle hardened. In the meantime Peter had started to walk on ahead. I hollered at him but he did not return. I tried to scare my driver by threatening to call the police. He just laughed. I thought maybe I should give him the extra 5 Yuan but was hesitant to do so, being loath to show the bundle of cash I carried. My next thought was to knee him in the crotch and get away from him. I realized he could overtake me quicker than I could walk and I was unable to run due to a prosthetic leg.

Luckily, he finally gave up and let me go on my way. I heaved a sigh of relief and caught up with Peter at the hotel entrance.

We enjoyed our days on the rest of the trip with no other occurrences of mischief.

41

TURKISH BATH

In May 2001, I took a four-week adventure tour called The Silk Route. With a group of fellow traveling adventurers, I took a train from Peking, China, across China, Kazakhstan, Uzbekistan and part of Russia, ending up in St Petersburg.

One of our stops was in Bukhara, Uzbekistan. This city was destroyed in the fourteenth century by Genghis Khan, an insatiable general with an army originating in Mongolia.

When one is on a tour with other travelers, one is usually constrained by the tour guide, who speaks the language. He will take you to the museums and the areas of interest. Most times, I go through museums ahead of every one else. The local guide knows too much and bores me to tears with so many details that I can't absorb and will forget before the day is out.

After a few days of sightseeing in Bukhara we had an afternoon to ourselves. So, what to do? Earlier, during one of our walks in the city centre, I had noticed, on a massive old building constructed out of basalt stones, a sign with a description of a Turkish bath. Taking a peak into the entrance, I discovered, with the help of someone speaking very broken English, that in addition to the steam bath they also gave massages. I was informed that I could make an appointment for the afternoon for $6.00 US. This I did, and looked forward to an interesting experience.

The ancient city was very intriguing and I needed to orient myself to its layout. I took a close look at my surroundings—the streets, the build

ings and other special land-
marks—so I could find the
bath building again. Right
after lunch I took a $2.00 taxi
ride from the hotel to within a
half a block of the bathhouse,
ready to keep my appointment
for a steam bath and massage.

Before leaving the hotel, I
had changed into a pair of
shorts and T-shirt. In addition, since I am a left below-
knee amputee, I changed from
my regular prosthetic walking
leg to a simple peg leg. This

Storytelling at the Blue Chair Café.

leg has a straight steel pipe with a round, flexible rubber stump, the size
of a large hockey puck, for a foot. It is what I use for showering. Off I
went, wearing my jaunty Canadian Tilley hat, looking somewhat offbeat.
I could tell that other pedestrians wondered or speculated how I lost my
leg. I did not care and left them guessing. This is me, take me as I am. In
a way it gave me status.

Arriving at the bathhouse I was shown where the clothes lockers
were. This turned out to be within view of personnel and others entering
the building. While undressing I realized I hadn't thought about bringing
a towel or an extra pair of under shorts or bathing trunks, so there I was
'buck naked'. The masseur lent me a thin worn towel and led me through
a low-ceilinged tunnel passage. The surface was slippery; I walked bent
over and held on to the masseur for dear life, fearing to fall or hit my
head.

We entered the steam room with a high ceiling, and he pointed to a
flat stone floor where I was to lie down on my flimsy towel. The floor
was extremely hot. Later I learned that they build a fire under the floor
from the outside. A fellow traveler from France joined me. We lay there
on our heated floor and chatted a bit, wondering how long we would

have to cook before the masseur would get to work on us. We were perspiring like horses after a run in a heat wave.

After about 15 minutes the masseur signalled for us to rise from that dungeon and moved us to a different part where we could recover by drinking water and splashing ourselves with it to cool down.

The masseur was now ready to go to work and had me lie down on my back on the flat stone floor in an area that was not so hot on the surface. He started to work on all my ligaments from head to toe. He did a good job massaging and pummelling all the body parts, until he reached my right arthritic knee. When he put pressure on it I cried, Ouch!"

"Problem?" he said—one of the few words he knew in English.

"Yes," I replied.

He let up on the knee and continued to other parts of the body until he got to the other knee and asked again, "Problem?"

I answered, "No".

He finished with the front, and indicated that I should roll over onto my belly, still on that measly wet towel. Lying face down, he worked me over starting from shoulder to arms and legs, asking me from time to time, "Problems?"

"No, no problem."

When he was nearly done he touched my back and repeated the refrain, "Problem?"

Thinking he was asking if I had back problems, I replied, "No." Before I knew what was happening, my masseur started walking all over my back! He was short, but still weighed at least 130 lbs and all I could do was gasp for air. I was unable to cry out, "Yes, problem!"

Fortunately he did not have a long walk and I was relieved when he came down from my by then tender body with the words, "You fini!"

I took a few deep breaths and wondered if my spine was still in good order. I thought perhaps they had cooked me in the steam room to have me tender and supple enough to walk on.

The masseur led me back to the locker room. I was holding on to him again, not wanting to slip on the wet stone surface. He lent me another worn towel to dry my body and pocketed $8.00 US. I supposed the increase from six to eight dollars was for the extra towels.

Turkish Bath

Leaving the bathhouse I bent over forwards and backwards a few times to check whether my spinal cord was still in one piece. I was happy to go outside into the cool air of nearly 30°C.

42

KOSOVO, 1999
(going on a diet)

Crossing the border into Alberta from our winter stay in Arizona one year, we stayed overnight in Lethbridge. Grace and I favour the Lethbridge Lodge because it serves excellent food and has good service. Also, upon crossing the border into Canada after a long trip, we like to celebrate our Canadian citizenship. We look forward to a leisurely, hot dinner, after driving 2400 kilometres in two days and living mostly on sandwiches and fruit.

Sitting down to dinner that evening, our thoughts were on our safe journey so far and on enjoying a nice dinner. At the same time, we were reminded by the news about atrocities in Kosovo: refugees were fleeing their homes with only their clothes on their backs, suffering from insufficient food. As we asked a blessing over our food we couldn't help but think of the horrors of war and that we were fortunate to have so much. One feels so powerless to help those people in desperate need, unable to anything but to pray that they share in God's goodness.

On this particular evening, I felt very self-conscious about our wealth in general, especially our abundance of food and that we have more than we need. It struck me that it was so easy to ask God to take care of those destitute refugees. What about our responsibility? What was expected of me?

When our dinner was finished and we went to our room, I felt bloated from all that rich food. Later, as I undressed for bed and looked in the mirror, I was not pleased to see my bulging midriff. Arriving home the next day, I weighed myself and was shocked to see that I had put on 10 lbs in the last few months for a total of 210 lbs or 95 kg.

It was at this point that Kosovo came to my mind again and how I probably overindulge in food that could be sent to those in real need. Moreover, being overweight might cause physical problems. Right there and then I realized that here was an answer to the prayer about helping out the hungry in Kosovo: go on a diet—eat less—and give more to foreign aid. I made a solemn pledge to start a diet and share more of my income. I wrote a cheque for much more than I would save on eating less food and drinking less alcohol.

It is easy to make a pledge, but hard to keep the promise. The hard part lay ahead. I discussed my resolve with my sister Mary (a nurse at the time). She, herself, was struggling with weight loss and gave me a diet plan from the hospital dietician. I got started right away.

This seven-day crash diet consisted mostly of eating soup, fruit and vegetables. The first day was not too difficult: for breakfast some fruit, mid-morning a bowl of soup, more soup for lunch, a third bowl later in the afternoon and one more at supper time, and in the evening some fruit. The second day: no fruit, just soup and green salads. The third day: fruit, soup and salad.

This was getting monotonous. Grace was feeling sorry for me. Sometimes she ate by herself so as not to tempt me or give me cause to cheat on my diet. To this point I had resolutely passed by any delicacies that had passed before me. By Day Three I had lost 4 lbs.

My prayer changed to a more intense giving of thanks for the food that I really didn't enjoy anymore. Still, Kosovo's hungry refugees kept me on track. I had flashbacks of our war days in the Netherlands when I was a teenager saw people begging for food. I expressed thanks for this experience, which heightened my awareness of our rich lifestyle relative to the many refugees in the world.

Day Four: I was allowed to eat bananas and drink skim milk. It was delicious, after all the dull soup. The soup lacked tasty meat stock; it contained only thin bullion, cooked beans, carrots, celery, a green pepper and some onions. I had now lost 6 lbs.

Day Six: lost 7 lbs. We had company. Besides salads and soups, I was now allowed beef with veggies, but no wine or other alcoholic beverages. I took a sip of wine from Grace's glass; Mmmm!

Day Seven: down by 8 lbs. This day I ate brown rice, veggies and the same boring soup. I ate a bowl of soup for breakfast and headed for church, bringing with me the envelope with a cheque for the Kosovo relief fund. After church I caved in and had a piece of cake and milk in my coffee. Man, oh man, it tasted good!

Lunch and dinner consisted of rice and salads, plus some unsweetened juice. Sunday evening I told Grace that I intended to continue the diet for four more days.

Next morning I was still only down 8 lbs and was disappointed; I had thought I would be down to my objective of 200 lbs.

I continued anew with the seven-day menu. On Day Ten I reached my objective of 200 lbs. For good measure, and still being in the 'groove' of the diet, I extended my regimen for two more days. But I did not lose another ounce. Just the same, we celebrated with a meal of beef stew and a glass of wine.

I was thankful for my health and wellbeing and intended to be more careful with what I took in, in the hope of dropping another 10 lbs. I praised God for giving me the perseverance to stick with my diet.

Fast forward. I was able to keep my weight in check, just below 200 lbs, for about four years. When my weight started creeping up on me again, I was introduced to the book written by Susanna Summers on how to lose weight and keep it off. I followed her advice and lost one to two pounds each week, until I was down below 180 lbs, feeling and looking better.

43

REMEMBRANCE DAY
(November 11)

June 6, 1944.

We all listened, clandestinely, to a radio hidden amidst sacks of seeds in our warehouse in Holland. There was good news on the radio: the great invasion of allied forces had landed in Normandy! We had longed to be delivered from Nazi forces that had subjugated all of Europe during the last five years. At this news, we were happy, to say the least; we were jubilant!

Fast forward: 50 years later.

Grace and I, together with my brother and his wife made a memorial trip to France and visited the coast of Normandy where that large invasion had taken place. We followed the stretch of coast, where the British, Canadians and the Americans had landed, from north to south. It was awesome. We did not realized, in 1944, what it was like to storm those well-fortified beaches.

The following day we went to visit one of the largest battle monuments, a cemetery where thousands of soldiers were buried. We looked over the massive gravesite. There was a large bronze statue, 22 feet high, with the following inscription in the granite floor: "The Spirit of American youth Rising from the Waves"

We shed our tears.

44

GREECE AND A DIGITAL CAMERA

In June, 2002, we went to Greece on a tour called "Following the Footsteps of the Apostle Paul". It was to be a fourteen-day excursion. Our itinerary included sightseeing on an air-conditioned bus for the first ten days and sailing the Mediterranean on a cruise ship for the last four.

Before leaving, I purchased a digital camera, then still a novelty. This new invention—taking pictures without film—seemed a good idea. The pictures can be downloaded into your computer and stored there for retrieval and may be printed, preferably on colour-photo paper. Furthermore, you can purchase a memory chip, choosing from various storage capacities according to the number of photos you may need on a particular outing.

Acquiring a camera is the easy part; learning its intricate capabilities is something else. The sales person is eager enough to show you how it works. Having practiced his sales pitch hundreds of times, he goes over it with lightening quick fingers, showing you all the different functions.

Unfortunately, I am not the brightest when it comes to mechanical stuff or reading the instruction manual. As a senior who had not kept up with new technology, I had a hard time absorbing all this rigmarole, but I hoped to find out more from reading the manual later, at leisure, in my easy chair. I thought I would be able to master it and did, in fact, try some shots inside our home. I liked the unique feature which allows you to delete any unwanted picture from the camera at will.

Before departing, I read some more in the manual and practiced shots in and outside the house. I experimented with the different settings: high resolution and low resolution, automatic flash, close-ups and distance shots. It dazzled my mind, but I thought I understood its functions now.

Some days later, off we flew to Europe, stopping off in Holland to visit our siblings and to get our biological clocks in tune with European time. While there, I practiced some more with the camera and was satisfied with my acquired skills in digital photography. The pictures had a sharp image. I was happy with this new toy.

Arriving in Athens some days later, I removed the smaller digital memory chip of 100 mega bytes (Mb) to a 300Mb memory chip, which would be more than adequate for the two weeks we expected to be there. The first day after our arrival we went to see the Parthenon, which takes quite a bit of uphill walking. You can see all of Athens from its height; very impressive. That evening we dined in a hillside restaurant opposite the Parthenon which had a splendid view of it, all lit up with lights. From our seats, we could take pictures of our friends with the lighted Parthenon in the background. What a perfect shot to show our friends back home!

At the end of each day, I would go through the photos I had taken and remove duplicates or any others unworthy of keeping from my artistic point of view.

We spent a few days in Athens, viewing many sights and museums. From there we traveled to Thessalonica and then on to Philippi, which was first settled in the Bronze Age, around 5000 BC. In 42 BC, the Roman army of Brutus and Cassius lost the battle against Octavia and Anthony, defending Julius Caesar's policy. The Roman ruins in Philippi, excavated many years ago, gave impressions of the Roman times. One could see where the market used to be and the crumbled walls of a basilica. Even a road was still visible. Not too far outside Philippi, we stopped to take pictures of a creek where Lydia, the seller of purple fabrics, was baptized by the Apostle Paul.

Heading southwards via Kalambaka on the return trip, we viewed some monasteries that were built high up in the mountains. They were not very accessible for me as I am a below-knee amputee. I could only take a picture from a distance, using the close-up feature of the camera.

Further south, crossing the Gulf of Corinth, we stopped at the city named Olympia, where the Greeks, at one time, held their athletic games. I noted that they had a very modest arena for their activities, relative to present day Olympic facilities worth billions of dollars. Also, the Greeks ran barefoot, whereas our athletes will spend a few hundred dollars on a pair of running shoes!

The weather stayed sunny and I left the camera set on automatic. This setting would allow me to shoot at will without having to fiddle around. It registered 100 saved photos in its memory chip so far, which I anticipated possibly using in a slide show.

On Day 10 we traveled eastward towards Corinth and crossed the Isthmus Canal, continuing in the direction of Athens. There we boarded a good-sized cruise ship. It would take us to different islands in the Aegean Sea. We steamed overnight to Ephesus, an Ancient City on the Turkish coast. Two thousand years ago it was one of the greatest trading cities in all of Europe, with about 250,000 inhabitants.

Ephesus was a very impressive place in history, a city having an infrastructure that supplied the city with running water from the hills near by. It supplied all the drinking and bathing water, plus a sewer system that ran through the bathhouse. This bathhouse had a row of stone toilets. Cameras were very active, photographing us as we posed there, sitting side by side. We speculated what musical sounds might have been produced there in the past, not to mention the aromas.

Other places of interest were the large library and the market place where the apostle Paul once preached about the false gods the Ephesians were worshipping. We saw the big amphitheatre were Paul was castigated by the silversmiths and artisans who were losing business, because he was speaking against idols made by human hands. For Bible readers, these places are referred to in the Book of Acts. Seeing them allowed me to visualize those recorded events.

On Day 11, we were back on our ship, steaming to the islands of Patmos, Rhodes and Crete. We anchored on the north shore of Crete, near Knossos, and boarded a bus that took us to the south shore of the island, to a fishing village with steep walkways and a path going upwards to another monastery. Grace and I did not make it to the monastery because, after walking up part-way, our legs were complaining. Instead, we turned around and found an idyllic restaurant and had a cup of coffee. In a nearby wall you could see, through an opening, flowering trees, with the Mediterranean Sea and a lighthouse in the background. It was great opportunity for a picture, with us sitting near the opening, so we asked someone to take a photograph of us with this gorgeous view. He was happy to oblige and took a picture of us with our camera. What a great shot! It should be something to brag about; surely we'd be envied for having had the opportunity to view this beautiful Island of Crete!

Time was getting on and we had to get going to catch the bus for our cruise ship. We didn't want to miss the boat. Later, sitting on the bus, there was time to review the pictures taken, so I went to sit in the back of the bus to be alone. I especially wanted to review the most recent pictures. I noted that they were not very bright. I realized I should have changed the setting from automatic to the flash position. How stupid of me, to miss changing the settings when shooting against the light! Intending to change the setting, I found I had forgotten how to do it. I clicked on the Menu button and other buttons until I found where it said, "Save" or "Delete" and asked "OK?" Yes, I wanted to save it and pressed "OK". In that split second, I deleted all 140 of our carefully selected, priceless pictures. Oh, what horror! I was dumbstruck and started sweating, wondering if it could be undone. No. Oh! Tears welled up in my eyes.

I felt defeated. I went to sit beside Grace again and told her about the mishap. She tried to console me, but the stupidity lingered in my mind. I couldn't imagine how to overcome this disaster, though I knew one should not walk around with a sombre, pouting face. I shared the mishap with another person and knew the word would get around that Francis was grieving.

When we came together at dinner that evening, no one raised the subject of my misfortune. They didn't want me to shed tears at the dinner table, I presumed. Most eyes were diverted from me, conversations with me too sensitive.

How could I break the spell? I had to face up to it. Think positive, I told myself, you did not loose an arm or a leg! I faced my dinner partners and asked for their attention, with the cliché, "I've got bad news and good news." All eyes and ears turned my way. Briefly explaining my misfortune, I followed it up with the idea of coming back and doing the whole trip over again. I raised my wine glass for a toast to a bright future. Oh, yeah? my inner mind said. Forget it, Francis, nothing doing.

45

BANGLADESH
(JANUARY 1991)

While recovering from an accident more than three years ago and trying to adjust to wearing prosthesis, I was bored to tears. The snow and slippery roads added to my distress. I was home-bound and feeling restless. I thought of Roy Berkenbosh with whom I had become friends when he and I were students at the Kings University College in Edmonton. Roy had been recruited to be a Field Representative in charge of a mission station in Bangladesh. He lived there now with his wife and four children.

I contacted him by post and asked if I might visit him and his family. I reasoned that it would be warm there and I would be able to move around outside if I so desired. I received a quick reply: "Yes, we would love to see you. Come on over."

There was no direct flight, as you can imagine. My flight was via Vancouver, Seattle and Thailand. In Seattle, I was given the option of cancelling my flight due to a warning, by unknown persons, for the airline not to fly to Thailand. To me it was a scare tactic; I believed it had to do with the possible invasion of Iraq by NATO forces. I ignored it. In fact, since I was using crutches I was driven in a wheelchair through customs at every stop. I accepted this service with a smile. Never had I been treated with so much respect. What a difference, though, for a man who used to travel easily with a backpack.

I arrived in Thailand after 33 hours. I took a two-night stopover in Bangkok which helped me to be relaxed, relatively speaking, when I arrived in Dacca, Bangladesh.

My host was waiting for me at the Dacca airport and drove me to his home in a district outside the downtown. It was a gated community; the entrance was secured by one of his day guards. The family home was spacious enough to put me up, although the housemaid had to vacate her room and, to her displeasure, share a bed with one of their daughters. Roy, his wife, and their four youngsters made me feel welcome. I, on the other hand, provided a respite from the local people and their customs; I brought news from home and some goodies not available in Dacca.

Roy was the Field Representative for the Christian Reformed Church World Relief Fund (CRCWRF) reaching out to people in agricultural areas. One of his jobs was to check the progress of the local managers in charge of training teachers in reading, writing and the practice proper hygiene. Their system was to attract intelligent women from among the poor, teach them to read and write, and send them, when qualified, into the very poorest neighbourhoods to teach others the same. This gave the poor the ability to read contracts from land owners, enabling them to discern whether or not the landowners were scrupulous. They could also read about better ways to raise crops. Becoming literate greatly improved their lives.

This kind of teaching takes a lot of patience and is very time consuming. It is also not necessarily welcomed. The local station managers were Christians, but called themselves Muslims. If the local people had known about their Christian faith, they would have ostracized the managers, to their own detriment.

Roy took me along to some of the small, outlying towns where substations were located. On the way out of town, whenever we had to stop for stoplights, there were beggars ready for a handout. Roy got to know the regulars and would often surprise them with something other than money, such as a plastic bag of grains, rice or some other nutritious foodstuff.

In the countryside, traveling with Roy in his sturdy, four-wheel drive SUV, I enjoyed the scenery. At one time, Roy and I had backpacked in the mountains; we both loved the outdoors. Some of what I saw along the way was new to me: small and large rice paddies; streams carrying water for the rice fields; rickshaws loaded with dry wood; and a bridge damaged from a rainstorm. We had to take a ferry to get across the river.

Every hour or so of driving, we stopped at some place for a cold drink. The locals would congregate around us and study our faces with suspicious curiosity to find out who we were and where we were going. Roy had taken lessons to learn the Bengali language and, with a smile, could give them enough information to satisfy them.

Arriving at each destination, we visited the school where lessons were in progress. We were introduced as benefactors from Canada who loved God, "Who has been good to us and Who wants us to share the good news with you". We had to be careful not to be seen as trying to convert them.

On another trip we went through a larger town and passed through a street market. Again, we felt that close scrutiny. Of course by then the war in Iraq had started and, being in a Muslim state, the people saw the West as the infidel, although Bangladesh did have a few hundred soldiers in Iraq. One fruit-seller in the market, with a picture of Saddam Hussein in his stall, looked at us with hatred in his eyes.

Our place to stay was provided by a friend. Supper was prepared, consisting of spicy rice and other concoctions. We ate with relish. The owner did not stay as he had appointments elsewhere.

Roy suggested going for desert in a downtown restaurant. It was getting dark and the restaurant was not well lit. We seated ourselves on a wooden bench. Roy suggested a local dish that tasted very sweet. I did not like it very much and left some of it. While sitting there we noticed some young men—you don't see women in those Islamic restaurants—watching, until one young man came over and asked us what we were doing around here. Roy tried his best to explain our business as benefactors, pointing out that "we are Canadian and friends with the Bangladesh people". They were not impressed with our story. Sensing possible controversy we decided to slip out of the restaurant and head for our sleeping quarters.

Undressing for the night and getting into bed, I found my stomach complaining. I stayed in bed for a while but then realized this was serious and headed for the toilet. It was a horrible experience: throwing up at first, going back to bed, 15 minutes later going back to the washroom and having it come out both ends. After going through that several times, the water for flushing the toilet ran out. Apparently the apartment owner shut off the water in the evening to prevent overuse. Fortunately, by then, my stomach was nearly empty. Also, there was a pail of water for emergency use which was just enough to wash my hands, have a drink and flush the toilet one more time. Thankfully, I slept for the rest of the night and felt normal in the morning.

Transportation for most people in town was by rickshaw. Roy showed me how to hire a rickshaw for going around the safe part of town, to the market to buy produce and so on. We both went for a haircut, which cost a dollar and included a massage of the neck and arms. They kept massaging until we asked them to stop and of course we paid them 2 dollars for our haircut.

Now that I was familiar with the neighbourhood I took a rickshaw on my own, while Roy went to another appointment. I had to use hand signals and learned to say two words in Bengali, the words left and right, to get the rickshaw puller to take me where I wanted. On the way back I decided to walk, using my cane for balance and reducing the weight on my prosthetic leg. I had not gone half a block homewards when I noticed three rickshaws following me. They thought this white man walking with his cane would never make it back. I tried to ignore them, but halfway to my host's home I gave up and hired one of them. It was so cheap that you could not help but pay double the price agreed upon.

Before returning to Canada, I left instructions for my crutches to be given to someone who was an amputee and was a using a stick to get around.

I had a good time with Roy, Grace and their children. I traveled back home with a satisfied feeling, knowing that Christians are donating several million dollars to the CRCWRF around the world and that it is a good investment. It was also good to see that all of the staff are receiving moderate incomes and travel in tourist class.

46

NEPAL

I used to be an avid backpacker and did most of my hiking in the mountains of Alberta. Occasionally, reading or watching a television show about Mount Everest, I would dream of going there someday and going partway up its 27,000-foot height to imagine some of what it takes to reach the top. In 1991, I had my chance. I was in Bangladesh for a week, and, as Mount Everest was only a good hour away by air, I decided to make a side trip to Nepal and get a close up view of the Himalayas.

It was a spur of the moment decision. Nevertheless, I had no reservations. My friend Roy, who was living in Bangladesh at the time, dropped me off at the airport.

Arriving there, however, I found there was no room on the flight to Nepal. I asked to be kept on a waiting list in case of a no-show. While waiting and looking around, I saw a large bunch of mostly young people sitting around on the floor, half asleep on their backpacks. Being curious, I mingled with them and asked someone who spoke reasonable English where they were headed. One of them responded that they were headed to Nepal, on a charted flight, but that the flight was booked solid. Then he asked me where I was from. I explained that I was from Canada and told about visiting our foreign mission station in Dacca. "Oh," he said, "I love the Canadians; they are helping us to reforest the hills outside of Katmandu." The hills had become bare from people harvesting the trees for cooking fuel. This young Nepalese man was excited to meet me and suggested I look for him at the arrival hall in the Katmandu airport. He would look after me and show me around.

Fortunately, I did get to board the next flight and, sure enough, he was waiting for me at the Nepal airport. I told him about my wish to see the Himalayan Mountains. "No problem," he said smiling, "Come and meet my sister who lives close by, then we will go to my town five miles away, called "Bhaktapur" and you stay with us overnight." I hired a taxi for five dollars to get there and arranged for the same driver to pick us up at 5 a.m. the next morning for a drive to a lookout at 8000 feet.

The man's home had at one time been a Hindu temple. The building had a stone face with an open entrance supported by pillars. The main floor was converted into a workplace for handicrafts. Everywhere, I saw various images of different gods made of wood. My Nepalese friend tried to explain the different types of gods to me and showed me which one was the most powerful god. I tried to find a way of explaining that we have only one God who rules the world without competition, but he was so animated and excited in his explanation that I eventually gave up.

The second floor contained the living room and kitchen where I was introduced to his family, his mother and five siblings. I was taken to my quarters on the third floor where I had to stoop deeply in order to enter; the door opening was only 5 ft high. Looking over the room, I saw a small table and chair and a small wooden bed with a thin blanket to sleep on and a second thin blanket for a cover. Not particularly soft on the ribs, I mused. It also occurred to me then, that I might need to visit the bathroom during the night, one or two levels below me. With my impaired mobility as an amputee, this could be a problem. I asked if he could arrange a facility in my room. Yes, no problem, and he brought me a pail.

He also brought me food, a dish filled with rice with veggies and a few slivers of chicken. After supper, he showed me through the neighbourhood, pointing out different buildings that he thought might interest me. Unfortunately, I was not too impressed with the old, messy and somewhat smelly back roads.

The next morning, the taxi we had ordered for 5 a.m. arrived punctually. The driver took us up a long, winding road up the mountain to the promised lookout. However, he made a small detour to pick up two young female cousins of my friend, pretty and fairly well-dressed but terribly smelly. Sitting in the front seat beside the driver I opened the window a little. I heard someone say, later, that their very different food intake may have been the cause of this scent.

While driving up the winding road, I observed the steep, barren, terraced hills. These would be subject to mud slides in a heavy rain, which explained the desperate need to reforest them.

Arriving at "the top of the world", we had a splendid view of the sun just creeping over the horizon, with a colourful sky over the Himalayan Mountains. Just fantastic! My wish was fulfilled and I was thankful for the opportunity to make this journey.

Returning to Bhaktapur, I dropped off my host, who was feeling ill and needed to go home. We said our goodbyes and I thanked him for his hospitality. The taxi driver wanted to stop here and there on the return journey to Katmandu for me to visit other sights, such as the Hindu temples. I thanked him but declined. I had had seen enough of Hindu or Buddhist temples. I get rumbling feelings in my heart, almost chilling, in those places that are so foreign to my Christian background.

He dropped me off at a restaurant near the airport and I invited him to join me for lunch. This time he declined, but he returned an hour later to take me to the airport. The total cost for the taxi for the day was $32.

I returned to Dacca and stayed two more nights with friend Roy and his wife, Grace, and their family. We feasted at a nice hotel for a goodbye dinner consisting of fried rice, pieces of pork and Asian spices, special the curry. I flew back the following day, with the satisfied feeling of a mission accomplished.

47

VICTORIA, B.C.

In March 2008, Grace and I went for a visit to Vancouver Island. We took a flight by West Jet from Edmonton. Renting a car, we headed for our Bed and Breakfast, Wintercott Country House, not far from the airport. We had been given a map and told that it was no more than 15 minutes, but it took us half an hour. The road signs on the island have room for improvement, we determined; more signs with larger letters would help. It was the same in the evening on our way to a restaurant. That time, darkness and a winding road added to the difficulty.

Our hosts were Peter and Diana Caleb, a couple originally from the UK. The English type breakfast they served consisted of smoked ham, sausages, and slices of cucumber and tomato. Another specialty was poached eggs with slices of smoked salmon. While enjoying breakfast, Peter, the cook, would entertain us with stories and opinions. Peter had a host of stories; at times we had difficulty leaving the table. To stop him I would stand up as a signal that it was time to end the conversation.

On Sunday morning we went to a Christian Reformed Church called Christ Community Church, a fairly large church. They were having a combined service with their sister church in Victoria. We arrived early, thinking it might be well-attended; best be early to find a seat before it gets packed. There was lots of room. I was told it used to be full 20 years ago, but not anymore; the younger generation is showing less interest.

While taking a seat on a bench near the back, I asked the person in front of me how old the church was. He did not know, but asked where we were from. I told him Edmonton. Then he asked, "Do you know someone called Francis Ruiter?"

"Yes, that is me!"

Surprised, he said, "I am Wim Shoemaker and was your neighbour in Andijk, where we were born."

I was flabbergasted; I had not seen him for 60 years and would never have known he resided here on Vancouver Island. But what a nice surprise! We had so much to share. His brother Wouter had been employed in my father's seed business for 45 years. He apologized for not being able to have us over for a visit—he had a houseful of visitors already—but we promised to keep in contact by email until we visited the island again.

Grace and I went to downtown Victoria to have a light lunch. We walked around Chinatown at first, but felt uncomfortable there when we came across a young couple sleeping on the sidewalk.

Instead, we found an old-fashioned café. It was not aesthetically pleasing to Grace, who was looking for a classier place, but to me it looked interesting and I coaxed her inside to observe the customers. It became a cultural experience. I could tell several people were regulars. There was a particular elderly couple, maybe 85 plus, sitting there at ease, enjoying a late breakfast. He was steadier in consuming his breakfast than his wife who struggled a little to control her fork. When they finished, they walked arm-in-arm across the street and entered the concert hall. The waitress confirmed my observations that they were regulars. There where other peculiar-looking types, young people wearing toques in 10°C temperature, for example. I then took note of a new arrival, an elderly person with a nice moustache extending past the corners of his mouth. He was wearing an old-fashioned cap and came in the door with a smile. Space was limited in this small café, but this old fellow became a doorkeeper, letting people in and out until his favourite place became available. I observed all this while enjoying my soup. I found it all interesting and felt touched with this experience.

From there we drove back to our B&B to have a nap. Afterwards, we moved to the sitting room to play cards together. Grace did most of the winning. At 5 p.m. we left to go to a restaurant called Piccolo, recommended by our hosts. It seemed all the good restaurants there have Italian food. Instead of choosing fish like the previous night, we ordered chicken with pasta for me and mashed potatoes and veggies for Grace. The wine was the same, but more expensive. We considered doing without the wine, but we had enjoyed it too much.

During the week, we visited the British Columbia Museum. It is three stories high and has very beautiful historical artefacts of B.C.

Since we had seen Butchart Gardens several times, we skipped it but went, instead, to visit Sidney and the fish market. It was very quiet. There were no ships unloading a fresh catch.

Then Grace started walking up and down the streets looking in the shops for I didn't know what. I just followed her in our car, parking here and there and waiting patiently for her to be ready to call it quits. She finally found something, a necklace with matching earrings.

The next day we went for lunch at Martin and Agnes Haasjes. Agnes is a cousin of mine. The Haasjes live about 50 kilometres north of Victoria, west of Highway #1. The last time we met had been about 18 years before. Now we had a good opportunity to update each other on our life experiences.

The lunch having been so rich, we decided, that evening, to go to Tim Horton's for a simple meal. We enjoyed chilli con carne with buns, and coffee. It tasted very good and it took no more than 20 minutes. The cost of it was hardly more than the tip for a meal in a fancy restaurant, like the Rosie and Med Grill (where it took us more than an hour to dine); at Tim's you don't break the bank going for dinner.

All in all, our week-long trip to Victoria was restful and memorable.

48

THE LONELY TRAVELER

There are times a person seeks adventure. It may be to relieve boredom or it may be to relieve stress. In my case it was both, but also, and mainly, it was my wanderlust. I enjoy reading adventure books and studying maps of far-away places. Travel movies get me exited; I always feel that I must see that place, go there.

My spouse, on the other hand, is satisfied with a short holiday. She prefers a country where the English language is spoken and western food is served and the hygiene is good.

Since I liked the idea of bumming around anywhere in the world, I would occasionally, with Grace's blessing, travel solo. When traveling on my own, going places where I was unable to speak the local language, I made sure I took a few paperbacks with me—fiction stories to pass the time. When I got really bored, I would lose interest in solitude and want company. Sometimes I got lucky and met a fellow traveler who spoke my lingo and we could share our experiences.

One time, in Rome, Italy, I got sidetracked. I had stopped for a pint of beer in a bar, when a man moved next to me on the bar stool to make conversation and suggested he take me to a nice place for a drink. It sounded good to me and I accepted a ride that took us a mile from the down-town area to a place where the lights were dim. There, my friendly Italian led me to a place where you went down several steps to enter a building, or the underworld, you might say. We were escorted to a table where a waiter was swift to take an order from my Italian friend who ordered a drink and, unbeknownst to me, invited more company. I was still disoriented, trying to figure out what kind of place I was in. Drinks were placed on our table, and a good-looking woman came to sit beside me.

Oh she was pretty all right, and very charming and attentive. She was a good listener, and her perfume was overwhelming; my senses were ambushed in an unsuspecting way. To be honest, my first reaction was, "Oh, what friendly company we are having."

After a few minutes' conversation, I became aware that this was not the place I had anticipated it to be, even though it had seemed so cozy at first. I looked for my Italian friend for explanations, but he was gone. My eyes went to the table where the waiter had placed a bottle of expensive champagne, together with a bill. Studying the bill, my face contorted. I realized I had been tricked. I was not as smart as I thought I was.

It was time for damage control. Before I had left my hostel, I had purposely put away my credit card and most of my cash as a precaution against pickpockets. I faced the waiter and asked where my companion had gone. He responded, "Oh, he left to see his girlfriend."

"Too bad," I said, showing him what was in my wallet. "I do not have enough money to pay this bill." Then I took the money out of the wallet, put it on the table, stood up and left before he could stop me. I managed to get out without being followed by a bouncer and took a deep breath of fresh air. Feeling relieved, I walked back to the downtown area, found my lodgings and slept soundly with no strange dreams. A thought that greeted me as I woke the following morning was, "Do not go places where angels fear to tread." Arriving home a week later, I told my dear wife that I had missed her, missed having her with me to share some of the sights I had seen.

I made no mention of the Italian bar incident. However, I could not hide this story for very long and related the whole thing some weeks later. Though she looked at me with questioning eyes, she graciously accepted my report. I felt relieved.

49

THE ARTIST

She is my schedule. There are set rules in our home from the time she rises in the morning to the bedtime hour in the evening.

Everything in our domicile is always perfectly in place. Each article of clothing from underwear to jackets is either perfectly folded and stacked in drawers or stored in closets. Chairs and cabinets are always placed in a certain spot or at a certain angle.

The contents of the kitchen cabinets look like a row of soldiers on parade. Pots and pans are neatly stored, and don't anyone displace them!

You will never see a speck of dust anywhere.

She is good at displaying and rotating artefacts of interest and other trinkets throughout our home. It is part of her artistic sense of beauty and charm. Her husband sometimes feels berated for is lack of insight on how to keep a dwelling in proper order. Over the last fifty years he has acquiesced to her suggested changes of both decor and behaviour: do not leave anything out of place; dress neatly; remove footwear when entering the home. It has caused some strife between us at times, but she is more joyful when all is in order and near perfection.

It is her perfection that has made her a good artist. This ability, which was evident from the time she learned to draw in her early school years, developed into a hobby after our children were married and living on their own. At that point, she took a course in different types of media from drawing to painting. She was mostly drawn to watercolour painting and became proficient and successful in her new world of art. Ironically,

Grace, the artist.

she has a difficult time deciding what is more important, keeping her house in perfect shape or taking time out to do watercolour painting.

Her husband has noted that, once she takes up her pencil and starts to sketch or takes up her paintbrush to follow through with the colours, she is in her element. She is in a state of total concentration when drawing or painting. Except for brief exclamations when she makes a small error in her work, there is total contentment. There is a feeling of quiet productivity and a peaceful aura around the house.

Her husband is in awe, not disrupting her except for a peek with a word of encouragement, which she needs to build up her self-worth and confidence. She has received many positive comments and won an art contest among senior citizens from ten similar facilities.

Looking back over our years as a married couple, I feel blessed to have contentment in our marriage. It could so easily be different. We are totally different in our makeup; I am extraverted and my counterpart is a bit withdrawn. This has certainly caused friction at times, but the positive attributes won out. It seems to me that we needed each other's strengths to complete each other and to meet each other's needs as well as the needs of our children.

My dearest put up with me when I lost patience. When I needed a break from my work routine and wanted to take off on a hiking tour or expedition, she accepted my wanderlust. It was not always to her liking. In fact, she managed to slow me down at times, which proved beneficial.

(Even more drastic measures were taken by angels who were in charge of me; they gave up protecting me from following the wrong course too many times. I feel I share Jonah's experience in the belly of the whale. Like Jonah, I was brought to my senses and straightened out. I lost a part of my leg while riding my bicycle; someone managed to hit me and catapulted me into a ditch. I went from being an athlete to a below-the-knee amputee, a devastating experience. I accepted my ordeal, not thankful for the accident but that God thought me worthwhile to be bothered with.)

I am grateful for Grace.

MY MEMOIR

Born in The Netherlands 1929
Small village, horticultural region
1940-45 Teenage years,
War, anxiety, curfews, fear
Grade six, teacher ex-sergeant, disciplinary
Grade eight, non-academic stream
Self-worth was impeded"
Restless, loved play and games
1948 British Columbia, uncle, mixed farm,
Horses and cattle
Winter, bush, timber, sawmills
1952 Edmonton, my sister
Encouraged to read, learned new words
Canadian National Railway
Applied and declined, employment,
Apprenticed, no pay, was hired
Telegrapher, one year, laid off
1954 Applied sales position
Seed company five years, felt appreciate
1959 Recruited, sold Life Insurance
Discovery, I could absorb information
Did well, built vocabulary
1979 Money, by itself, no gratification
Applied to enter college, part time
Discovered my potential, sweating
Had the words, not right order, red ink
1987 Bachelor of Arts, in History
2003 Arizona College, read a Poem
Professor, much praise, shed a tear
Here I am, Thank you Lord

ABOUT THE AUTHOR

Francis travelled from Holland to Edmonton on the troop ship, the Kota Inten in April of 1948. A week later he moved to his uncle's small range in Houston B.C. where he was employed for two years as a farm hand. After that, he became a Lumber Jack. In 1952 he moved back to Edmonton and, after a number of occupations, he ended up as a Life Insurance Agent for 30 years. He was forced into early retirement after a bicycling accident, which left him an amputee. This represented a dramatic life change. Prior to the accident, Francis was an athlete who ran marathons, could bike a hundred kilometres on a given day, who loved backpacking, and who canoed the Coppermine River to the Arctic. After his recovery, however, he started to swim and he is thankful that he is able to swim to keep in shape.

CPSIA information can be obtained at www.ICGtesting.com
Printed in the USA
LVOW132312040612

284622LV00005B/23/P